WINNING CHESS
Tactics & Strategies

Ted Nottingham,
Al Lawrence &
INTERNATIONAL MASTER
Bob Wade

Sterling Publishing Co., Inc.
New York

DEDICATION

To the late Decima Douie, tenth daughter
of Sir James MacDouie (Governor of the Punjab)
and beloved history lecturer at the University of Hull

ACKNOWLEDGMENTS

Thanks to Allan Lewis and his son Jon for preparing the disk so thoroughly.

Sources include *Masters of the Chessboard* by Richard Reti (McGraw-Hill 1932), *Grandmasters of Chess* (Norton 1981) by *New York Times* music critic Harold Schonberg, *How to Force Checkmate* (David McKay 1947), "White Knights of Reykjavik" by Prof. George Steiner (*New Yorker* 1972) (Faber and Faber 1973), *The Batsford Book of Chess* (Batsford 1975) by Bob Wade, OBE. "The Merchant and the Arab" is based on a story by M. Jokai from Sakmat.

Also by the Authors:
  Chess for Children (1993)   *Playing Computer Chess* (1998)
  Winning Chess Piece by Piece (1998)   by Al Lawrence & Lev Alburt

Edited by Claire Bazinet

Library of Congress Cataloging-in-Publication Data
Nottingham, Ted.
      Winning chess: tactics & strategies / Ted Nottingham, Al Lawrence & Bob Wade.
          p.   cm.
      Includes index.
      Summary: Presents tactics and techniques for playing chess, including openings, middlegame and endgame strategies, forks, pins, skewers, and examples from the games of world champions.
          ISBN 0-8069-9956-X
      1. Chess for children Juvenile literature. 2. Chess problems Juvenile literature.
    [1. Chess. 2. Chess problems.] I. Lawrence, Al. II. Wade, Robert Graham. III. Title.
    GV1446.N6941999
    794.1–dc21   99-20300
                                                                                      CIP

10   9   8   7   6   5   4   3   2   1

First paperback edition published in 2000 by
Sterling Publishing Company, Inc.
387 Park Avenue South, New York, N.Y. 10016
© 1999 by Ted Nottingham, Al Lawrence & Bob Wade
Distributed in Canada by Sterling Publishing
% Canadian Manda Group, One Atlantic Avenue, Suite 105
Toronto, Ontario, Canada M6K 3E7
Distributed in Great Britain and Europe by Chris Lloyd
463 Ashley Road, Parkstone, Poole, Dorset, BH14 0AX, England
Distributed in Australia by Capricorn Link (Australia) Pty Ltd.
P.O. Box 6651, Baulkham Hills, Business Centre, NSW 2153, Australia

Sterling ISBN 0-8069-9956-X Trade
                0-8069-9332-4 Paper

CONTENTS

PART ONE
Far Away and Long Ago   4
The Merchant and the Arab   4
An Arab Position in Modern Times   5
Charlemagne's Queen   6
The Duel for the Queen   7

PART TWO
Openings   12
A Dream Start   12
Legal's Mate, 1750   14
Played in Paris, 1923   17
Best Save the Queen   21

PART THREE
The Fork   26
Knight Forks   26
Chess His Mother Tongue   28
J. R. Capablanca Plays the Fork   29
Capablanca's Knight Checkmate   32
Judith Polgar Plays the Fork   34

PART FOUR
The Pin   38
Pinning   38
One Pin After Another   40
A Devastating Pin   42

PART FIVE
Discovered Attack   47
Garry Kasparov   48
A Discovered Check   49
Nigel Short   53
A Discovered Attack   53
A Charousek Double Check and Mate   58
Nunn Plays a Discovered Attack   59

PART SIX
The Skewer   62
Kasparov Skewer and Discovered Attack   65

PART SEVEN
A Mating Race   71
King and Two Bishops Vs. King   71

PART EIGHT
Improving Piece Play   81
The Bishop   81
The Rooks   85
The Queen   87
The Knight   89
The King   92

PART NINE
The Endgame   93
Harry Pillsbury, an American Master   93
Pillsbury Plays the Endgame   94
Abe Yanofsky, a Canadian Prodigy   108
At Fourteen, Abe's Tight Corner   108

PART TEN
A Game to End All   114
Rudolf Charousek   114
A Dazzling Finish   116

SOLUTIONS   122
STRATEGY TIPS   123
CERTIFICATE   125
INDEX   126

PART ONE

FAR AWAY AND LONG AGO

The Merchant and the Arab

A Spanish merchant traveling a lonely road did business from town to town. One day he came across an Arab sitting in the middle of the road with a chess board.

Curious, the merchant asked, "Why are you sitting here alone playing chess?"

"Oh, I'm not alone," said the Arab.

"But I don't see anyone with you."

"That is," the Arab replied, "because I play the great Allah, the One who is everywhere!"

"You have a powerful opponent, then!"

"Yes, but a fair one."

"And is He winning?" asked the merchant.

"It seems so. Can you see how I can avoid being checkmated by His next move? It will mean I cannot play anymore today."

"Why not?" asked the merchant, puzzled.

"I will have lost all my money," replied the Arab.

Stunned and not believing his ears, the merchant said slowly, "You and Allah play chess for money?" He had never *ever* heard of such a thing.

"Yes. See, here I lose twenty gold pieces."

"But wait, how do you pay Allah?"

"Oh, of course Allah doesn't take the money Himself. He sends some honest holy man who takes it from me and gives it to the poor. That is the same as giving it to Allah. And, since I have indeed lost, you must be the man Allah has sent today. Here, do Allah's bidding and take these twenty gold pieces."

The merchant, not as honest or as holy as he might have been, was delighted.

Weeks later, again traveling that road, the merchant shook his head at the thought of the Arab who played chess with Allah. Suddenly, in the middle of the road, there again was the Arab, sitting alone with his chess board.

"Is Allah winning today?" asked the merchant, pulling his wagon up alongside.

"No," replied the Arab, happily. "In fact, in one more move I shall checkmate Him, and win a hundred gold pieces!"

"And however will Allah pay you?"

"Oh, of course Allah doesn't pay me Himself. He sends some honest man who will give me what I have won! Today," the Arab finished, "you must be the man Allah has sent to pay me the hundred gold pieces."

An Arab Position in Modern Times

The Arabs of the ninth century were the first great people to enthusiastically take up the game of chess. The Caliphs of Baghdad loved it. Over a thousand years later, an end-game problem by al-Adli, dating from that early time, occurred again—in a 1945 game in Storkovenhagen, Denmark, during a game between chess players Jorgensen and Sorensen.

Here is that recurring position. White mates in three. Do you see how? See the solution given upside down below.

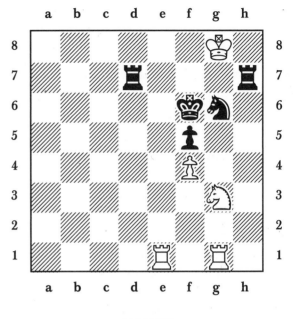

WHITE
Jorgensen

Solution:

1 Ng3 – h5+ Rh7 × Nh5

2 Rg1 × Ng6+ K × Rg6

3 Re1 – e6 checkmate

A BIT MORE OF HISTORY

European kings learned of chess from the Arabs, and it was not long before they, too, fell in love with the game. Chess flourished at Camelot, King Arthur's court in England. Legend has it that King Arthur, Queen Guinevere, Sir Lancelot, and the court wizard, Merlin, all played chess during the time of knights in steel and bewitching ladies in steeple hats. But it is from the court of Charlemagne the Great that the following story comes.

♛♛ DID YOU KNOW? ♛♛

Known as the Lucena manuscript, the oldest existing printed book on chess mentioned castling in 1497. Castling, that special same-time moving of a king and rook, was not known in the Arab game of chess. Lucena's work, published in Spain, was titled *Repetición de amores y arte de Axedres* and was actually divided into two sections: one half was on chess; the other half, on love!

Charlemagne's Queen

"Sir, your queen desires your visitation and to be acquainted with this stranger."

Shakespeare—*Henry VIII*

Galienne dressed plainly in white silk, the simple lines standing out amidst all the lavish displays of gold and ermine popular at Charlemagne's court. She moved quickly but with poise through the assembled crowds; after all, as wife to Charlemagne, she was queen.

Galienne's eyes caught sight of the theatre area, where jugglers tossed gleaming razor-sharp daggers, acrobats perched precariously on poles and Saracen girls balanced on fast-spinning balls. The entertainment would go on all day, non-stop, but Galienne's tread did not slow and her mind was on the tournament.

Garin was to fight this day. Galienne enjoyed the jousts, with the huge, heavy French horses, barrel-bodied, pounding the ground with their thundering hooves. She thrilled at the sound of splintering lances and enjoyed watching the ladies throwing glances at the knights. Today, as queen, it fell to her to receive and reward the tournament winner. She hoped that it would be her favorite, Garin.

Garin was everybody's favorite and, as the crowds expected, so it turned out to be. Garin unseated his opponent with the first blow of his lance. Garin then defeated knight after knight after knight, leaving no doubt who was victor of the tournament.

As Galienne moved from the viewing stands to the reception tent to receive and reward the winner, her heart beat with excitement. Garin soon approached and knelt before her. After awarding the prize, Galienne spoke casually, "You did well in the joust, but do you play chess?" And so Garin agreed to come to court, at Galienne's request, for a game.

When Garin arrived, instead of having the board readied for a game, Galienne confessed feelings for him. Garin was shocked. He didn't know what to say or do. He adored his queen, but his heart belonged to another. And Galienne was, after all, wife to Charlemagne, Emperor of all Europe!

Garin's face paled. "I'm sorry…" he began in a whisper. Surely this queen would understand if he did not return her love. Instead, Galienne stiffened. How dare this, this *lowly* knight reject *her*! Her beauty turned ugly as her eyes turned cold. Then she turned slowly and swept from the room.

When Charlemagne heard about it, he vowed that such an insult to his queen would not go unpunished. Summoning Garin, he challenged him to a duel at chess under the following terms. If Garin won, the knight would have the queen to wife, and his kingdom as well. If Charlemagne won, he would have Garin's head! Garin quickly saw that his position was desperate. Even if he won, he did not love the queen. He also knew that he could not take Charlemagne's crown. And if he lost…his fate was unthinkable!

What happened? Well, the game went *somewhat* like this. (This is a modern version of the legendary game, because in Charlemagne's day pawns could only advance one square on their first move, the queen only one square, and the bishop only two squares—which would not help you to learn chess today.)

The Duel for the Queen

A s in the historic game, Charlemagne here plays White and Garin plays Black.

1   e2 – e4   e7 – e5

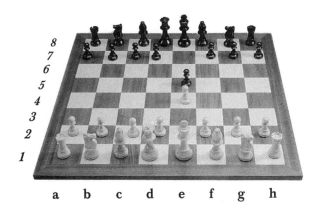

Charlemagne and Garin both move their center pawns forward in this opening.

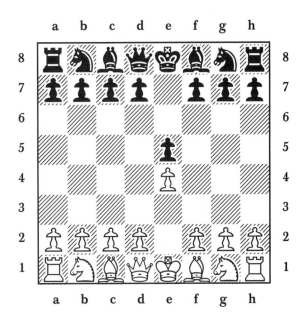

2   Ng1 – f3   Ng8 – f6

Both players then bring out their knights.

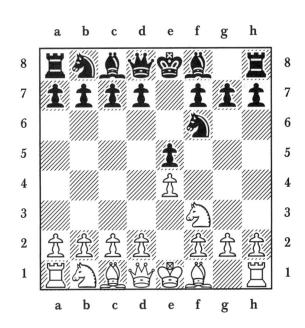

3 Nf3 × e5 Nb8 – c6

Charlemagne plays to go a pawn ahead. Garin brings his pieces out quickly.

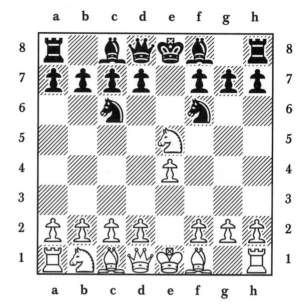

4 Ne5 × c6   d7 x c6

Both Black's bishops are now ready for play.

5 d2 – d3   Bf8 – c5

Charlemagne protects his pawn, but look! Garin has two pieces out; Charlemagne has none.

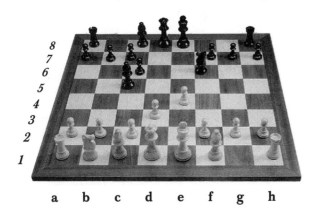

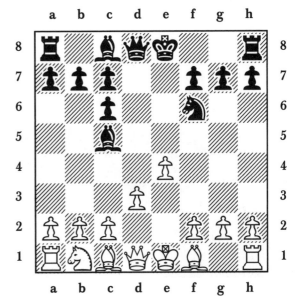

6 Bc1 – g5   Nf6 × e4

At last Charlemagne has got a piece into play and Garin is going to lose his queen.

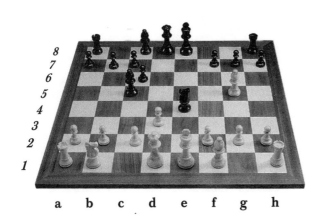

7 Bg5 × d8   Bc5 × f2+

Yes, he has, but now comes a check to which
White has only one reply.

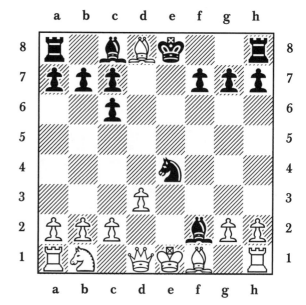

8 Ke1 – e2

White's only move.

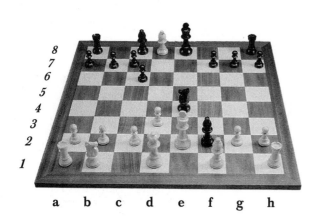

8 .....   Bc8 – g4 checkmate

And now Garin brings his bishop out to give
check and checkmate to King Charlemagne.

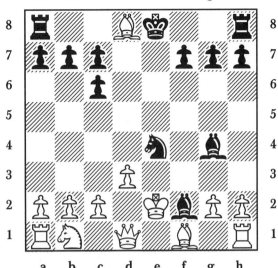

What happened then? Garin's steady gaze
met his king's. "Sire," he said, "I seem to have
forgotten the stakes of the game." He found
himself holding his breath.

Charlemagne frowned. Then, ever so slowly,
came the response, "Strange. The details have
left my mind, also." Then the Emperor smiled
suddenly—a broad smile that dissolved all the
tension. "I love a sportsman," Charlemagne
added, "and you certainly are one. Henceforth,
you are to be known as Garin of Montglane.
Come, Baron, let us be friends." Charlemagne
and Garin did become firm friends...but it had
been a very close call.

Photo by Jami L. Anson, courtesy U.S. Chess Federation, New Windsor, NY 12553

PART TWO

OPENINGS

Today we know a lot more about chess opening theory than Garin and Charlemagne could have known. We know, for example, that you should try to move a different piece with every move. Right from the start, you should move to get your whole army into play.

A Dream Start

Think of your chess board as a map with a fold across the middle, and each half of the board as a country on either side of a river. Although there are many ways to cross the river, the best place to do that is in the middle. Now, imagine there's a bridge there. When you start a game, you want to try to get as many of your pieces as possible into position to cross that

bridge into your enemy's territory. (Of course, you can count on your opponent to also be doing the same.)

Most openings are ways to try to do just this. As you improve your game, you will learn openings that attack first around the side, but most of the fighting will take place at the middle of the board, on your way to and crossing the bridge!

On the next page we give you only a White-side position, to help you see more clearly what we mean. Remember, your pieces are usually at their strongest in the center. Your king should be *castled*—moved to the side and *away* from the center and, at the same time, moving a rook *toward* the center. In this dream start, White's pieces are perfectly placed and are ready to attack the bridge.

♔♕ DID YOU KNOW? ♕♔

The folding chess board was invented by a priest! It was in 1125, at a time when the Church authorities very much disliked the game. Bishop Guy of Paris even excommunicated (banned from the Church) any priest caught playing chess. One such enthusiast,

after some thought, devised a less obvious playing board—one that looked simply like two books lying together. The idea of the folding chess board quickly became very popular, and you will still see many chess boards made in this way.

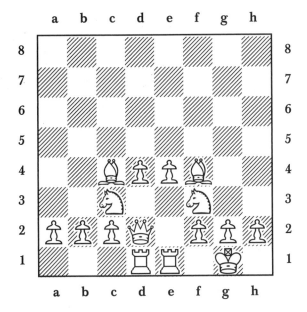

This dream position took just ten moves. See if you can work out what White's moves may have been up to this point.

As we said, your opponent is also trying to get *the* perfect start on his side of the board, and some of those moves will interfere with your ideas and stop you from following your plans for a dream start. An opening is the result of a player trying to find the best way to get in those first ten moves. There are hundreds of different ways to proceed, and there are whole books available that concentrate on only a single way! The great players are always trying to find better ways to play those first ten moves.

THE RUY LOPEZ

Here is an opening after only four moves. It is a variation on the start of one of the world's oldest chess openings, known as the Ruy López.

Can you see how White and Black made their first four moves? See the solution below.

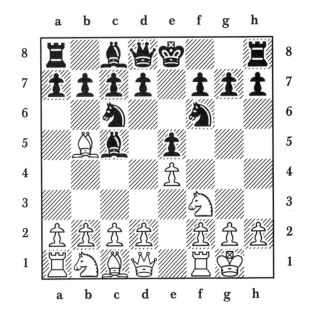

It's the Ruy López Berlin Defense variation.

Solution:	1	e4	e5
	2	Nf3	Nc6
	3	Bb5	Nf6
	4	0-0	Bc5

♛♚ DID YOU KNOW? ♛♚

The Ruy López opening dates from a work known as the Göttingen Manuscript, written in Latin in 1500 by Lucena. Ruy López, a Spanish priest, later wrote about the opening in a book which was published in 1561, so the opening was named after him.

Legal's Mate, 1750

The game by Charlemagne and Garin we showed you earlier can arise from a number of positions. What follows here is probably the most famous example. It was a game played in 1750 by the famous French chess player Sire de M. de Kermur Legal and an opponent by the name of Saint Brie. The game provides a number of surprises to watch out for.

Here, at right, is the position of the game as de Legal prepares to move.

WHITE   **BLACK**
de Legal   **Saint Brie**

De Legal makes his move.

1 Nf3 × e5

Saint Brie, playing Black, leaps to the bait.

1 .....   Bg4 × Qd1

He captures the white queen.

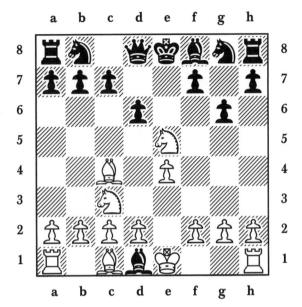

Now it's de Legal's turn.

2 Bc4 × f7+

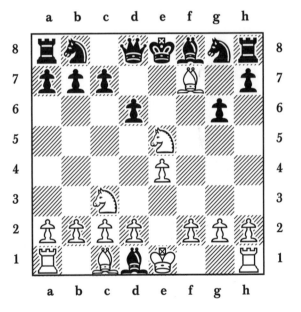

2 .....   Ke8 – e7

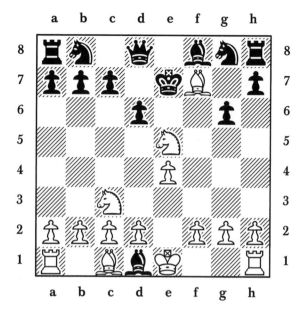

3 Nc3 – d5 checkmate

Be alert. Don't make the mistakes shared by
Charlemagne and Saint Brie!

Played in Paris, 1923

Here is another interesting game to learn from. Played in Paris in 1923, this short game was between two very strong players: Amédée Gibaud, a five-time French champion, and Fred Lazard, a champion turned chess journalist. It begins:

WHITE	BLACK
Gibaud	Lazard

1	d2 – d4	Ng8 – f6
2	Nb1 – d2	e7 – e5
3	d4 × e5	

The pawn attacks the black knight.

3 .....   Nf6 – g4

The knight is now ready to take back the pawn on **e5**.

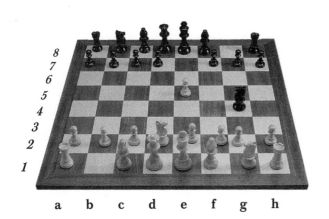

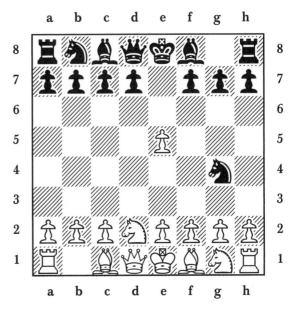

4 h2 – h3

Not a useful move: no piece comes into play.
Indeed, White's move leads to disaster.

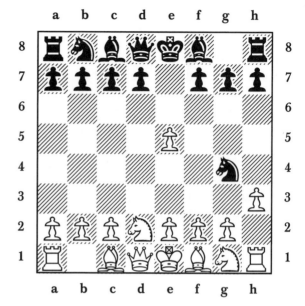

4 .....   Ng4 – e3

Attacking White's queen. Where can he go?
Nowhere.

5 f2 × e3

No choice: he had to take the attacker. But now Black can check.

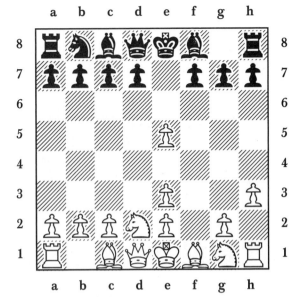

5 .....   Qd8 – h4+

What can be done to block the check?

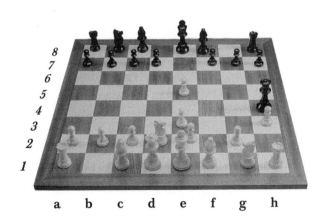

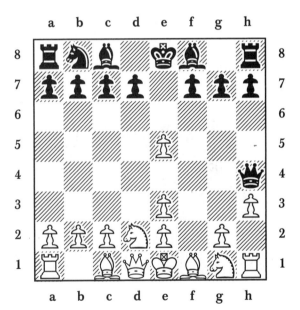

6 g2 – g3

Here's the only move that will block check.

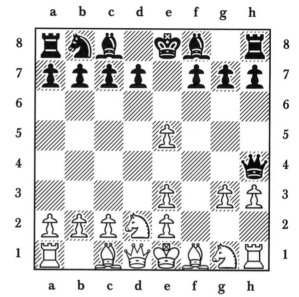

6 .....   Qh4 × g3   checkmate

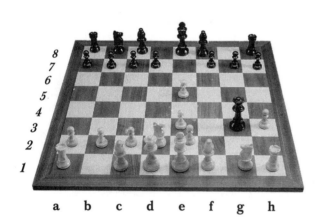

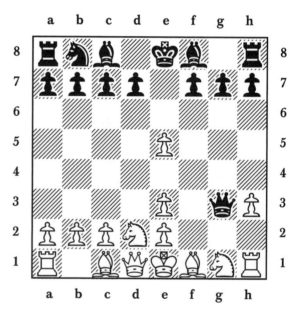

Best Save the Queen

Don't bring your queen out too early. The queen is the strongest piece on the board and, after the king, she is easily the most valuable. Be careful about bringing her into battle too soon. She may herself become the target of an attack. Let's see what happens in the following game.

The opening moves are:

WHITE	BLACK
1 e2 – e4	e7 – e5

This is a very common way for chess games to begin. Both players stake out claims in the center and provide outlets for their queen and king bishops.

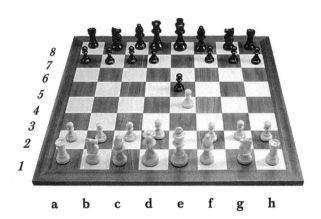

Photo by Jami L. Anson, courtesy US. Chess Federation, New Windsor, NY 12553

2 Bf1 – c4   Qd8 – g5

Black's strongest piece enters the battle alone.
She becomes a target for the white pieces.

3 Ng1 – f3

First, the knight comes out to attack. The queen
eyes the pawn on **g2** greedily.

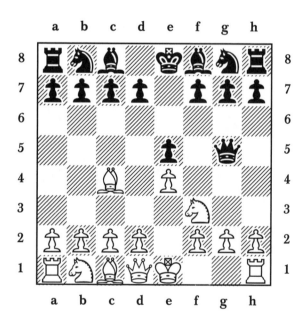

3 ..... Qg5 × g2

The queen grabs the white pawn. But watch now as the white rook comes out of the corner to attack her.

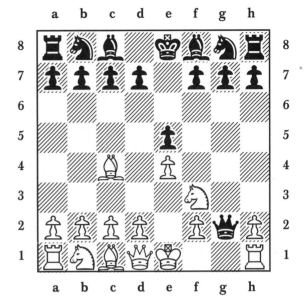

4 Rh1 – g1

The white rook is protected by its knight. White has now brought three pieces into the fray: the bishop, the knight, and the rook. The black queen has only one safe move.

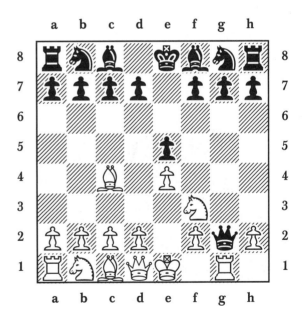

4 ..... Qg2 – h3

White could take the pawn on **e5** with the knight, but there's also a chance to attack the black queen.

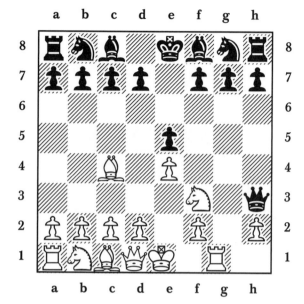

5 Bc4 × f7+

White seizes the pawn on **f7** with the bishop and gives check to the black king. What is the plan?

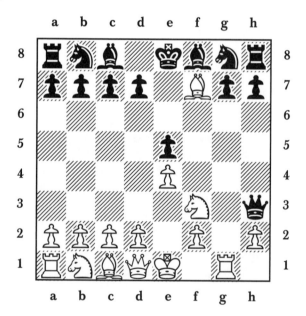

5 ..... Ke8 × f7

Black moves immediately to capture the bishop on **f7**.

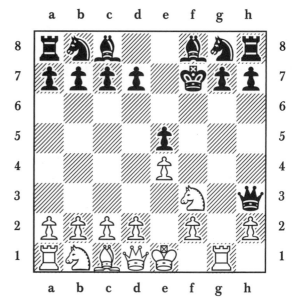

6 Nf3 – g5+

Black didn't see the danger. Do you? Look, White's knight can give check, forking Black's king and queen. It's a royal fork! Once the king moves out of check, the white knight will take the black queen. It came out dangerously early and it has been lost.

PART THREE

THE FORK

Knight Forks

The Douglas and the Hotspur, both together
Are confident against the world in arms.

        Shakespeare—*Henry IV Part 1*

Can you see how the knight can fork in the following cases? First, we have two examples of the royal fork. The white knight moves to attack the enemy king and queen at the same time in both diagrams.

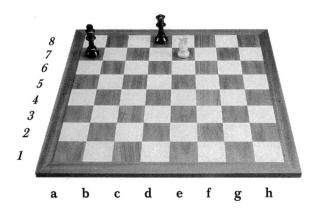

Solution:
Ne7 – c6

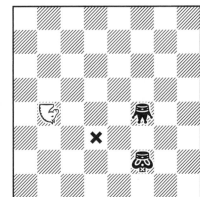

Solution:
Ng5 – e6

Now the black knight moves to fork the queen
and the rook. Can you see how it does, in each
of these two cases?

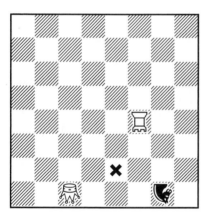

Solution:
Nb8 – d7

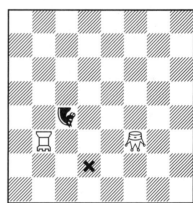

Solution:
Nf5 – e7

Chess His Mother Tongue

José Raúl Capablanca was a near-perfect chess machine. His outstanding results in international play early in the twentieth century are still held in highest esteem. When, in 1924, Capablanca lost a game to Richard Reti at a chess tournament in New York City, the *New York Times* headlined this newsworthy defeat:

CAPABLANCA LOSES FIRST GAME SINCE 1916

He was to chess what Louis Armstrong was to jazz, the Beatles to pop music, Pélé to football—simply the best.

Stories abound about "Capa." Once, while crossing the Atlantic on a great liner bound for New York, the chess legend was challenged to a game by a man full of himself who did not know who Capablanca was. Capablanca said he could play "a little."

"That's all right," the self-appointed ship's champion conceded. "In fact, I'll give you a queen start." Capablanca promptly accepted the man's offer, played the game a queen up, and lost!

"I'm very good," the man boasted. "I often give my opponents a queen start and win."

"Oh?" Capablanca said. "How about another game? It seems an advantage to play without your queen, so I claim that advantage now."

His opponent shook his head, then shrugged and agreed. If Capablanca could not win *with* a queen up, how could he expect to win without one? This time Capablanca won.

"Funny," said Capablanca, speaking to the large crowd that had gathered to watch the play, "chess is an easier game without the best piece."

Another great story, this one by Pedro Saavedra, tells of Capablanca's playing chess for his soul against the Devil. Before the Lord of the Underworld's final winning move, he asked his opponent, "What little deed would you like me to perform before I collect your soul?"

"With the touch of a finger, turn your king into a gold piece with a diamond crown," said the Cuban.

The Devil silently placed his finger atop the white king. Capablanca could hardly believe it! The wooden chess piece turned into solid gold and, beneath the Devil's finger, a large diamond appeared on top of the golden king, forming a magnificent crown.

But Capablanca composed himself, looked up at his opponent, and enjoyed saying, "You have touched your king, Sir. You have to move it."

Photo courtesy of www.chesscafe.com

Capablanca playing simultanous games

♛♚ **DID YOU KNOW?** ♚♛

José Raúl Capablanca is the most famous chess master to have given a simultaneous display in London's House of Commons. One of his opponents was Bonar Law, who was at the time Prime Minister of England.

J. R. Capablanca
Plays the Fork

Let us now look at a real sample of Capablanca's wizardry.

In 1935, in Morgate, England, Capablanca played a German gentleman by the name of Jacques Mieses. This was the position, at right, before Capablanca's eleventh move. He was playing White.

That was when the following possibility arose…

WHITE	BLACK
Capablanca	Mieses

11 Bc4 × e6

…a move which one biographer says "deserves to be known as the Capablanca Sacrifice." The move also occurs in Capa's games against the German master Ewfim Bogolyubov and against the Hungarian Kornel Havasi.

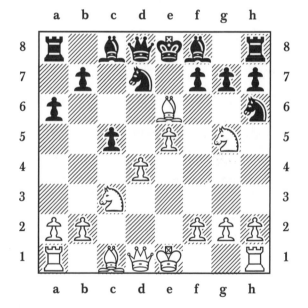

♞♞ DID YOU KNOW? ♞♞

Jacques Mieses [it's pronounced MEE-sees] had a keen sense of humor. Once, while in New York, Mieses was asked, "Are you Mister Meises [MY-sees]?" He replied, "No, I am Meister [My-stir] Mieses [MEE-sees]." ("Meister" is the German word for "Master.")

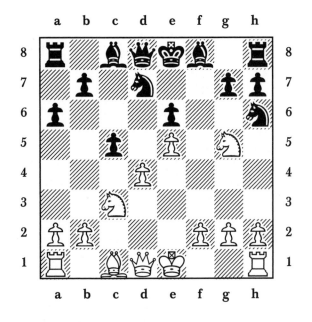

11 .....　　　　　f7 × Be6

12 Ng5 × e6

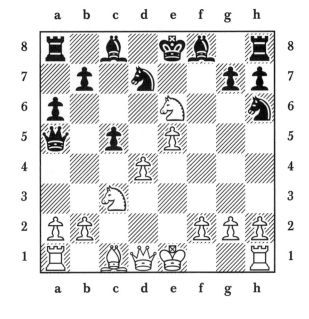

12 .....　　　　　Qd8 – a5

13 Bc1 – d2

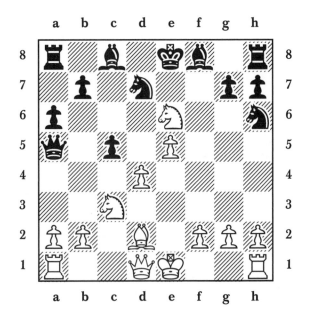

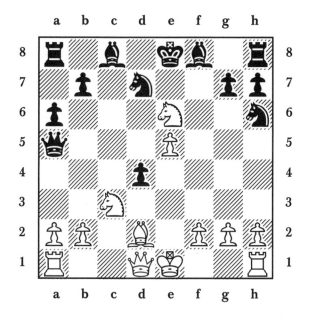

13 .....   c5 × d4

14 Nc3 – d5

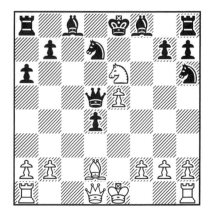

And *if,* **14 ..... Qa5 × Nd5**

then, **15 Ne6 – c7+**

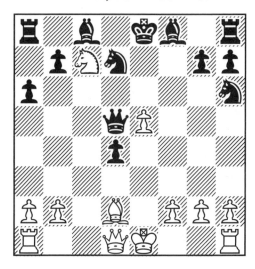

It's a royal family fork: king, queen and rook all under attack! Can you see it? Although Mieses did not fall into this trap, he lost nevertheless.

NOTE: The same fork will also occur if, instead of: **14. ..... Qa5 × Nd5**, Mieses plays: **14. ..... Qa5 – b5**, the only other move for the queen.

Capablanca's Knight Checkmate

It is very difficult in chess to calculate many moves ahead. Checks to a king or checkmating threats make it easier to do by limiting your opponent's choices.

The knight, besides providing for some devilish forks, can also deliver stunning checkmates. Now let's watch a master at work with the knight. We are going to show you a series of forcing moves by Capablanca.

Capablanca is playing White and it is Black's turn to move. At right, Capablanca threatens checkmate with **Ng5 – f7** and also with **Qh4 × h7**. Black plays...

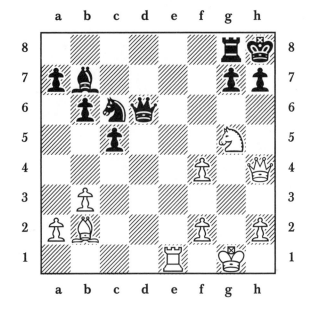

1 .....   Qd6 – g6

This stops the white knight from moving: it is now pinned along the "g" file against the white king. Despite this, White gives checkmate in two moves.

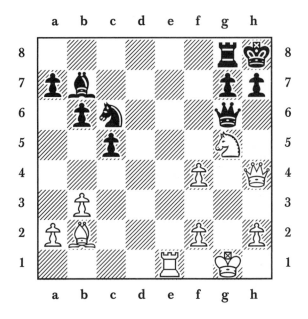

2 Qh4 × h7+

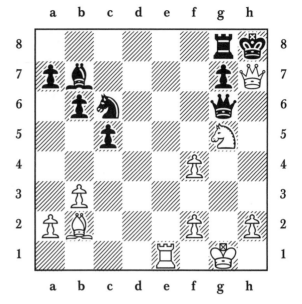

There is only one reply to this move. The king cannot take, as it would then be in check from the knight.

2 ..... Qg6 × Qh7

White has given up—we say "sacrificed"—his queen. Now, can you see the checkmate? Have you noticed that the white knight has suddenly become free to move again?

3 Ng5 – f7 checkmate

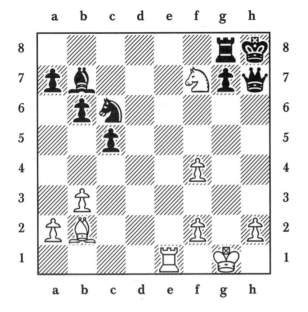

The black king is boxed in—called "smothered mate."

Judith Polgar
Plays the Fork

(The entrance of the Cell opens, and discovers FERDINAND and MIRANDA playing at chess.)
Shakespeare—*The Tempest*

In Buenos Aires in October 1994, eighteen-year-old Judith Polgar played in an impressively strong tournament that included FIDE (*Fédération Internationale des Echecs*) World Champion Anatoly Karpov and most of the world's best players. The final tournament table (at right) reveals how she performed, brilliantly, against the world's top men. Her progress has slowed a little now, but Judith Polgar still remains a serious threat to the dominance of men in world chess.

In a position from that tournament shown at right opposite, Judith, playing Black, sets a fork trap for Alexey Shirov. What happens if Shirov's queen should take Polgar's queen? If the black king does, there is an excellent fork that is also checkmate. Are you able to see it?

Judith Polgar

Buenos Aires, Argentina – October 1994

Name	FIDE rating	1	1	2	2	3	3	4	4	5	5	6	6	7	7	8	8	
1 Salov, V.	Gr. 2710	*	*	½	½	½	1	1	½	1	1	½	½	½	½	0	1	9
2 Anand, V.	Gr. 2720	½	½	*	*	½	0	1	1	1	½	½	0	½	½	1	1	8½
3 Ivanchuk, V.	Gr. 2695	½	0	½	1	*	*	½	½	0	½	½	1	½	½	1	0	7
4 Polgar, J.	Gr. 2630	0	½	0	0	½	½	*	*	½	½	1	1	1	1	½	0	7
5 Karpov, A.	Gr. 2780	0	0	0	½	1	½	½	½	*	*	½	½	½	½	1	½	6½
6 Shirov, A.	Gr. 2740	½	½	½	1	½	0	0	0	½	½	*	*	1	½	0	½	6
7 Kamsky, G.	Gr. 2695	½	½	½	½	½	½	0	0	½	½	0	½	*	*	1	½	6
8 Ljubojevic, L.	Gr. 2580	1	0	0	0	0	1	½	1	0	½	1	½	0	½	*	*	6

Average FIDE rating, grade 2693 (category 18)

Shirov vs. Polgar, J., Buenos Aires, 1994

The Polgar sisters (*left to right:* Sophia, Judith and Susan) at 1992 U.S. Chessathon

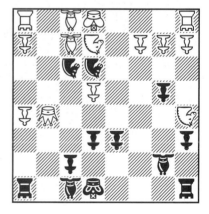

Solution: If Qg2 × Qg5, then Judith Polgar plays Ne5 – f3 checkmate.

TEST YOUR PROGRESS: FORK

On these pages are six positions for you to solve. Remember what you have just learned about the fork when you are trying to find the answers. First, try finding the solutions without using a board. Then set up each position and see if you can work it out without touching any of the pieces. After all, if you were playing in a match, you would have to *move* any piece you touched, even if it was the wrong one!

(Solutions on page 122)

Photo by Jami L. Anson, courtesy U.S. Chess Federation, New Windsor, NY 12553

1. Black to move

A knight fork wins material. Can you find it?

2. Black to move

A black check allows a winning fork.

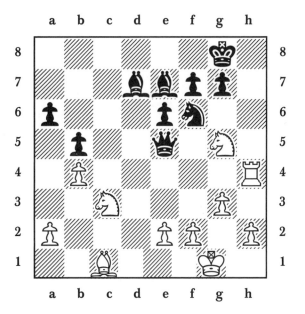

3. White to move

Remember Capablanca's royal family fork? Can a white queen capture set one up here?

4. Black to move

Can you make the white king or queen move so Black can make a winning knight fork?

5. White to move

White is down in material, but a clever check leads to a fork, winning the queen. What move?

6. Black to move

Black cannot take the knight or he will lose his queen. What happens if he takes the rook?

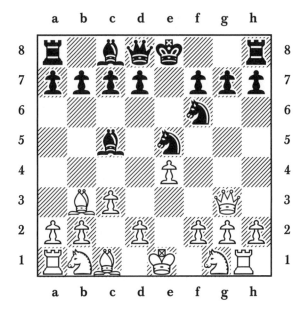

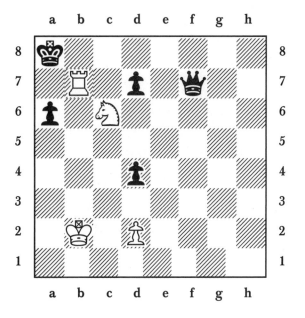

PART FOUR

THE PIN

And God forbid a shallow scratch should drive
The Prince of Wales from such a field as this.

Shakespeare—*Henry IV Part 1*

Pinning

If you attack an enemy piece that is shielding a more valuable one, you pin it. If your opponent should move the pinned piece, he is immediately exposed to a serious attack on a valuable piece.

In the board diagrams below, you can see that the white bishop on **e2** can move to the **f3** square, and so attack Black's rook. That's a good move. But look what also happens. If the rook should move from **d5**, White will be able to take the queen behind it! The black rook is said to be pinned against the queen.

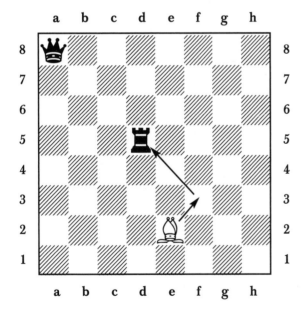

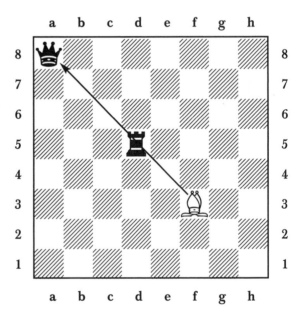

In another position, shown below, the rook can be pinned against the king by the white bishop. Do you see how? If the rook is pinned in this way the rook *cannot* be moved, since this would leave the king in check.

Now, on the board just below, can you see how the black rook on **a1** can pin the white knight against its king?

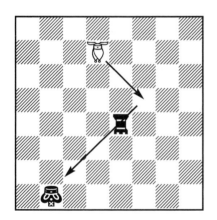

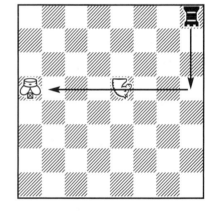

Solution:
Be2 – c4

Solution:
Ra1 – a4

One Pin After Another

The starting position with White to move.

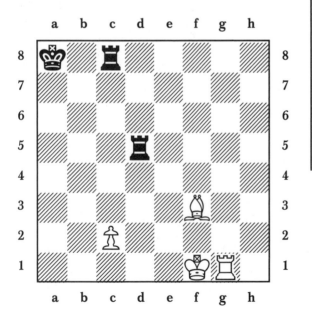

White plays **Be2 – f3** to pin the rook at **d5**. The rook on **d5** is now pinned and cannot move.

Black hits back. The move **..... Rc8 – f8** pins the white bishop against its king.

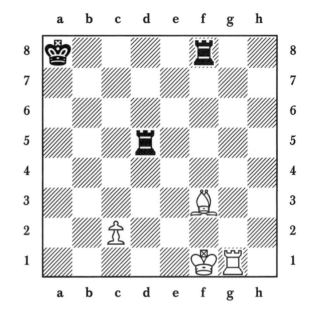

Finally, White pins the black rook at square **f8** against its king by moving: **Rg1 – g8**.

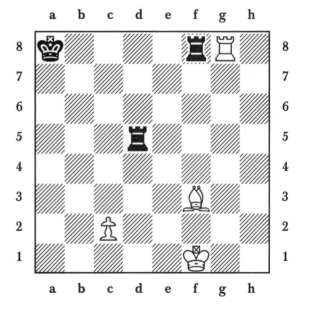

Black plays **.....** **Rf8 × g8**. The black rook *has to* take. But now, note that the white bishop is unpinned!

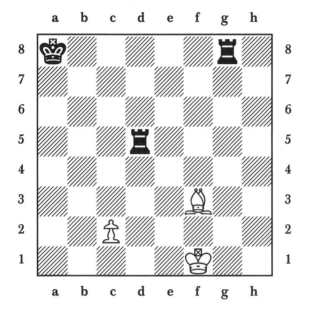

The bishop makes his move: **Bf3 × d5+**. It also forks the other rook. Some pin!

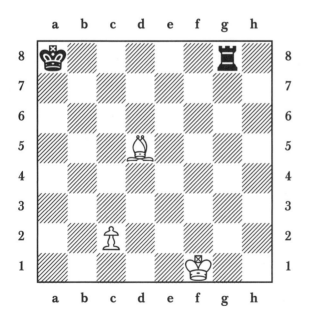

A Devastating Pin

In the moves that follow, White demonstrates beautifully the power of the pin to achieve a checkmate.

The position is at right and it is White's move.

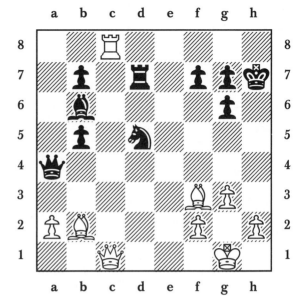

The white rook moves to attack the black king.

1 Rc8 – h8+

Black *must* take this rook.

1 ..... Kh7 × h8

The black pawn on **g7** must stay to protect the
black king from White's bishop at **b2**. It is
pinned to the h2 – h8 diagonal. Where can the
white queen attack?

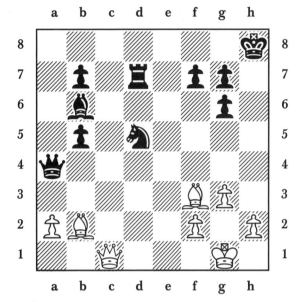

2 Qc1 – h6+

The pinned pawn cannot take it. The black king
must move.

2 ..... Kh8 – g8

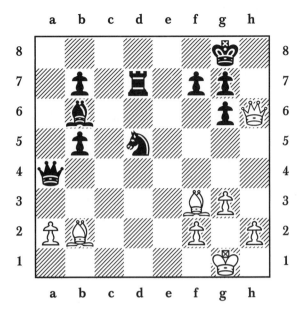

And now the white queen gives checkmate, using that faraway bishop for support by...

3 Qh6 × g7 checkmate

It is the end of the game. The king cannot be moved because of the white queen, and the queen cannot be taken because of the bishop. White has won! It is not all wizardry—if you understand the power of the pin, you can play these moves, too.

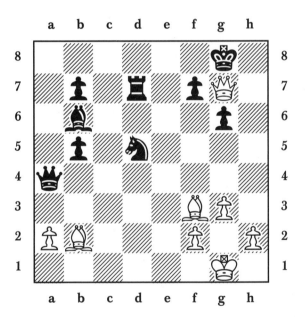

TEST YOUR PROGRESS: PIN

On these pages are six more positions for you to solve. Just like last time, what you have learned in this section on pins will help you to find the answers. First, try them without using a board. Then set up each position and see if you can work it out without touching any of the pieces.

(Solution on page 122)

Photo by Jami L. Anson, courtesy U.S. Chess Federation, New Windsor, NY 12553

1. Black to move

The white king and queen are on the same diagonal. Can you see the pin that helps Black win?

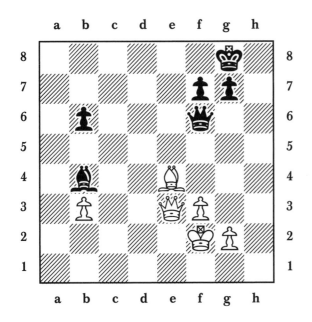

2. Black to move

White's pawn on **f3** is pinned by the bishop on **h5**. How can Black use this to win a piece?

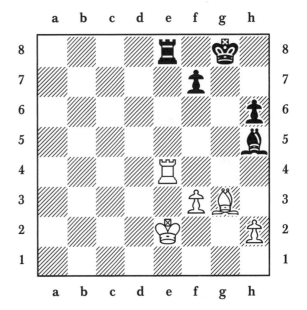

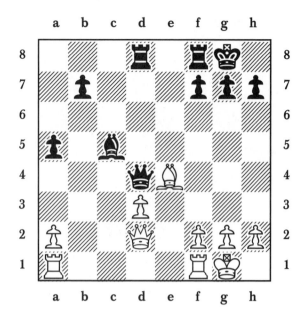

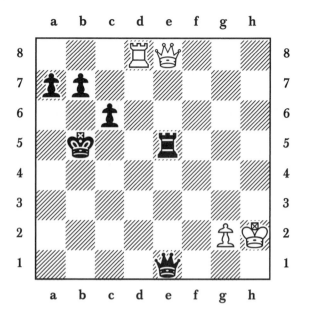

3. Black to move
White thinks his bishop is safe. Why isn't it?

4. White to move
White's rook is pinned and Black's queen is pinned. Can you find White's winning move?

5. White to move
White can win either the rook or the queen. How?

6. Black to move
Can you see why White loses his bishop?

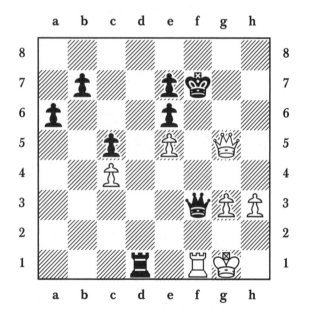

PART FIVE

DISCOVERED ATTACK

From this day to the ending of the world
But we in it shall be remembered
We few, we happy few, we band of brothers
                    Shakespeare—*Henry V*

In this section we are going to look at examples from the games of four masters of the chessboard: current champion of the World Chess Council (WCC) Garry Kasparov, his 1993 London challenger Nigel Short, Britain's clever John Nunn, and Rudolf Charousek, a tragic young player of long ago. Their games all provide demonstrations of what we call "discovered check."

Photo by Jami L. Anson, courtesy U.S. Chess Federation, New Windsor, NY 12553

Garry Kasparov

And learn a while to serve
Where kings command

Shakespeare—*Henry VI*

A world champion since 1985, when he was age 22, and the highest-graded player ever, Garry Kasparov has an air of invincibility that was possessed only by José Capablanca and former world champion Bobby Fischer before him. He is perhaps the strongest world champion of all time. He is certainly the richest.

In million-dollar matches against Anatoly Karpov in Moscow's Hall of Columns, against Nigel Short at London's Savoy Theatre in the Strand, and against Viswanath Anand on the top floor of the twin tower World Trade Center in New York City, Kasparov has not only made himself rich, but has often demolished human opposition.

In 1996 in Philadelphia, in another million-dollar challenge, he was pitted against the giant IBM computer "Deep Blue," which was able to calculate at fifteen billion moves a second. When Kasparov lost his first game, the media interest around the world was intense. In spite of playing two more games of the six-game match to draws, Kasparov finished up the easy winner by three games to one. Kasparov as representative of the human race had triumphed over the machine. But he, and humanity, were living on borrowed time.

In May 1997, an improved version of IBM's Deep Blue again challenged World Champion Garry Kasparov in New York City. This time, Deep Blue became the first computer to beat a reigning world champion under tournament conditions. The giant supercomputer won with a score of 3½ to 2½.

Most chess experts agreed that Kasparov was a much better player than Deep Blue, but that Garry was too worried about his opponent being a computer. He played too defensively. Then in the crucial last game, with the score tied, Kasparov's nerves cracked, and he made mistakes not expected of a world champion. Since IBM has ignored Garry's challenge to a rematch, it remains to be seen whether a computer can beat a human playing his best!

Dark and handsome, and always sporting expensive suits, Kasparov has political ambitions, hoping perhaps one day to be President of Russia. He has certainly been the strongest force in world chess in the last part of the twentieth century.

Garry Kasparov vs. Viswanath Anand

Photo by Jerome Bibuld, courtesy U.S. Chess Federation, New Windsor, NY 12553

We are going to look here at a game he played against Guy West, USSR–Australia, in a match by telex when Kasparov was only fourteen. It is not as good as thirteen-year-old Bobby Fischer's game against Donald Byrne in the 1956 Lessing–Rosenwald tournament in New York City, when Bobby played the "Game of the Century," but it is still a very good game.

A Discovered Check

The Kasparov–West game was played by telex machine and started this way:

WHITE	BLACK
Kasparov	West

1	e2 – e4	c7 – c5
2	Ng1 – f3	Ng8 – f6
3	Nb1 – c3	e7 – e6
4	d2 – d4	c5 × d4
5	Nf3 × d4	Bf8 – b4
6	e4 – e5	

Attacking the knight (see diagram at right).

6	.....	Nf6 – d5
7	Bc1 – d2	Nd5 × c3
8	b2 × c3	Bb4 – f8
9	Bf1 – d3	d7 – d6

10	Qd1 – e2	

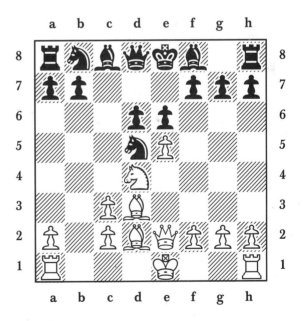

Here, in diagram at right, is the position after White's tenth move. White has moved more pieces off the back row and into play, so must have the better chances of winning.

10 .....   Nb8 – d7

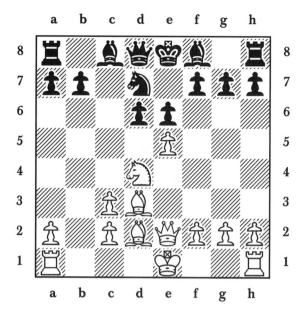

11 Nd4 × e6

This knight is trespassing. It has the impudence to attack the black queen. What happens *if* Guy takes it?

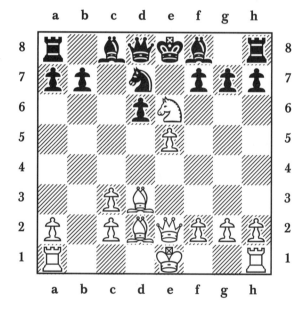

After Guy's capture with **11 ..... f7 × e6**, Garry would unleash the attacking team of his queen, two bishops, and advanced pawn by moving **12 Qe2 – h5+**. The black king now open, the game could then go:

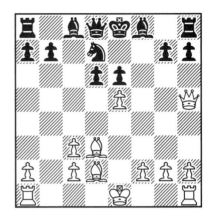

12	g7 – g6
13 Bd3 × g6+	h7 × g6
14 Qh5 × g6+	

The last move would drive the black king to **e7**, after which Garry would have skewered the black king and queen like a shish kebab with **15 Bd2 – g5+**, inflicting heavy material loss. (We'll show you more about "skewers" in the next section.)

Guy West didn't like that possibility. He did not take the knight but instead moved his attacked queen to square **b6**.

11 .....   Qd8 – b6

12 Ne6 – c7+

Checking the black king and attacking a rook.

Now, look carefully at the position. You can see that West can play queen takes knight (**12 ..... Qb6 × Nc7**).

Let's imagine that he does.

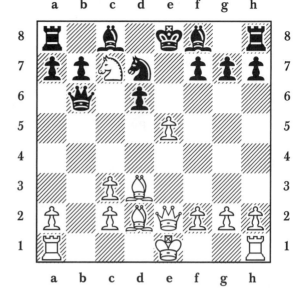

After **12 ..... Qb6 × Nc7**, Garry would play **13 e5 × d6** with "discovered check," as we say.

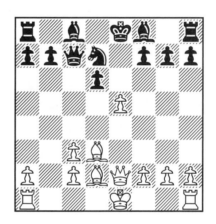

The black king, attacked by the queen, must be saved. The white pawn is attacking Black's queen. That queen would be lost, so Guy, instead of playing **12 ..... Qb6 x Nc7**, must move his king out of check. The knight then simply takes the black rook. This would be too much for Guy to make up, so he resigned the game.

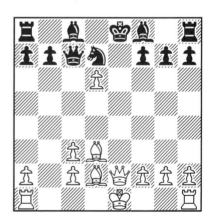

Nigel Short

Nigel Short is Britain's best-known player. In 1993 he had earned the right to challenge Garry Kasparov for the world championship at the Savoy Theatre in London. The first Englishman to play for the world title since Howard Staunton 150 years before, Short lost heavily to Kasparov by 6 games to 1. So did Viswanath Anand two years later in New York, so there was no shame to the loss.

Nigel Short learned to play chess in Manchester Schools Chess Association. By the age of eight, he was on board two in their under-11 team, and Leonard Barden, one of the heads of England's youth chess, then predicted that Nigel would become world champion. By the age of twelve, he was playing in the British championship, easily then the youngest person to have qualified. In this championship, he succeeded in beating ten times British champion Jonathan Penrose!

A Discovered Attack

Here is a game by Nigel Short, playing White, when he was twelve in a challenge at Charlton, London, against Max Fuller.

Max must keep his queen ready to stop Nigel from giving checkmate. This is what both Max and Nigel saw, and why Max resigned the game.

BLACK
Max Fuller

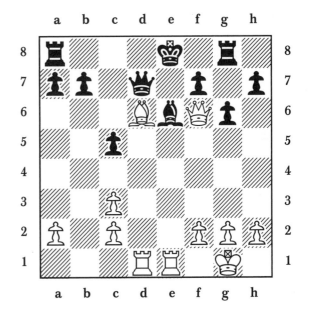

WHITE
Nigel Short

1 Bd6 × c5

This discovers an attack by the rook on the black queen. Now it's easy.

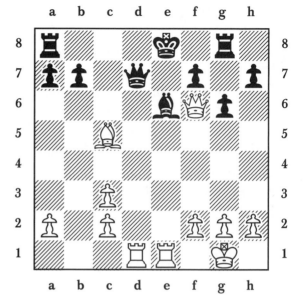

1 ..... Qd7 − c7

The queen moves to the side, away from the rook.

2 Re1 × e6+

Nigel breaks down the last defense.

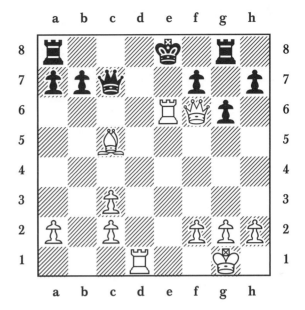

2 .....   f7 × Re6

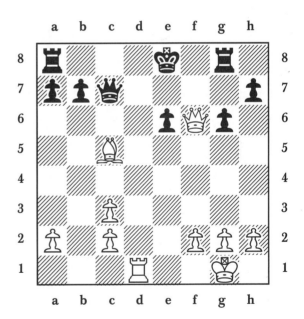

3 Qf6 × e6+

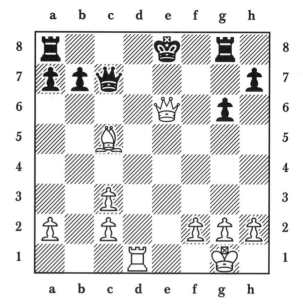

3 .....   Qc7 – e7

The only block Max has, but it is of no use.

Remember: Be sure to learn all the elements of attack. Learn to be alert to discovered attacks from *both sides*— those you could make and the ones your opponent might direct against your own pieces.

4 Qe6 × e7 checkmate

Two months later, Nigel would play in the British championship final tournament, easily the youngest player ever to qualify. There he would beat Dr. Jonathan Penrose, the ten-times former title holder, and achieve a rating performance from his eleven games of British 200 (2200 on the International Scale—a master's rating).

For reading practice, the moves of this entire game are given below in a short form of algebraic notation—only the piece's *arrival* square is given.

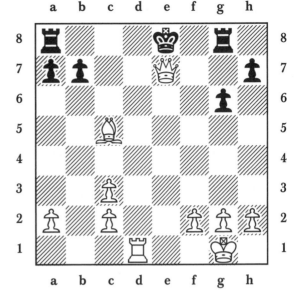

	WHITE	BLACK
	Short	Fuller
1	e4	c5
2	Nf3	Nc6
3	Bb5	Qb6
4	B × c6	Q × c6
5	0 – 0	g6
6	Nc3	Bg7
7	d4	d6
8	d × c5	d × c5
9	Bf4	B × c3
10	B × c3	Q × e4
11	Qc1	Bf5
12	Re1	Qa4
13	Qe3	Qc6
14	Ne5	Qc8
15	Nc4	Be6
16	Qe5	Nf6
17	Nd6 ch	e × d6
18	Q × f6	Rg8
19	B × d6	Qd7
20	Rad1	resigns

Nigel Short

A Charousek Double Check and Mate

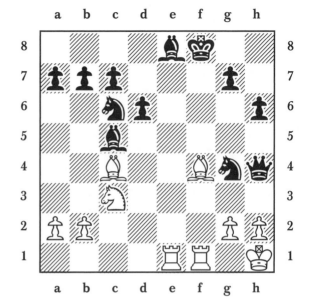

Do you remember that discovered check happens when a piece moves and another piece that was "hidden" is then found to be giving check? You may have noticed it yourself by accident! A strong version of discovered check can occur when the piece you are moving *also* gives check. This is then called double check.

Can you see how, in the position at right from a famous informal game between a champion Rudolf Charousek and J. Wollner in Hungary in 1893, Charousek, playing White, gives discovered check, which is also double check and checkmate?

You will find this complete, dazzling finish game, at the back of this book.

Nunn Plays a Discovered Attack

John Nunn is one of Britain's strongest chess players. A brilliant mathematician, he was admitted to Oxford University at the age of fifteen, at the time the youngest undergraduate to enter the famous university since Cardinal Wolsey in the fifteenth century.

In this example of discovered check, played at the 1986 Chess Olympiad in Dubai, a United Arab Emirate, John Nunn plays Black against Alonso Zapata of Colombia. The position is as below, and it is John's turn to move. Do you see how he can discover an attack from the white queen and win it?

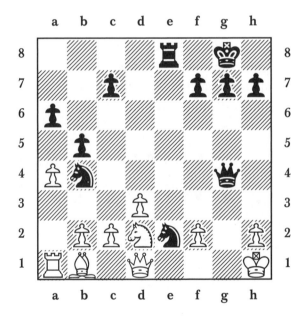

The black knight seems to be pinned. If it is moved, White can simply take Black's queen with the white queen.

However, the black knight can be moved in such a way that White has no time to take the black queen. How?

Look at the position again. What squares can the knight move to?

John Nunn makes his move.

1 .....   Ne2 – g3+

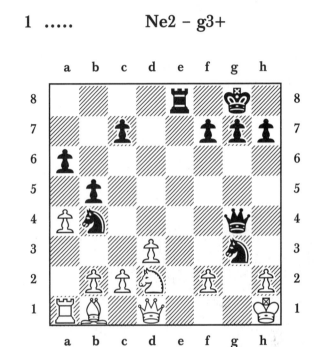

The white king must move out of check, and so allow John's black queen to capture the white queen.

TEST YOUR PROGRESS: DISCOVERED CHECK

Here are six more positions for you to solve. Once again what you have learned in this chapter will help you to find the answers. First of all, try them without using a board. Then set the position up and see if you can work it out without touching any of the pieces.

(Solution on page 122)

Photo by Jami L. Anson, courtesy U.S. Chess Federation, New Windsor, NY 12553

1. White to move
Look here for a white knight move that mates Black's king.

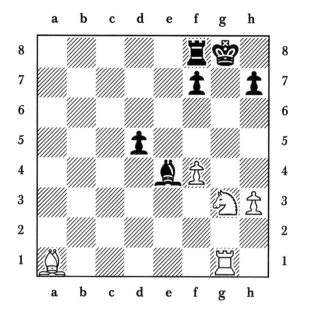

2. White to move
Can you see a discovered check that lets White win the black queen?

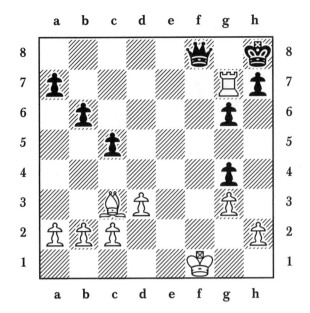

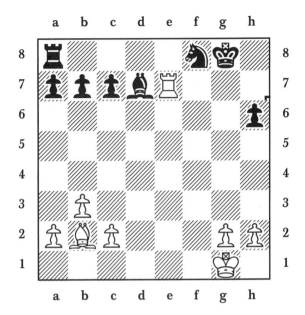

3. White to move

White is in check here, but a discovered check gives him a winning position.

4. Black to move

If Black's pawn on **e3** could move, there would be a discovered check. What can Black do?

5. White to move

This famous position, called a "mill," uses discovered checks. White plays **Re7 – g7+**. How many pieces can he win by just repeating checks?

6. White to move

Can you see why **.....** **Qf2 × g2+** wins?

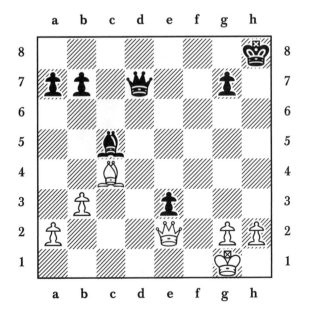

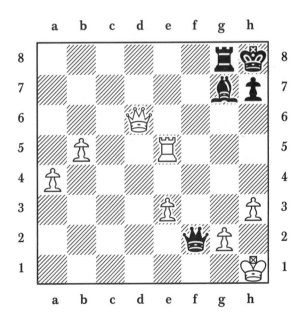

PART SIX

THE SKEWER

Remember how, in Kasparov's game, he threatened to shish kebab his opponent's king and queen? A skewer is a situation in which a valuable piece is attacked and forced to move, leaving another piece to be taken.

We'll show you first a rook skewer. Here, the white rook can move into position to skewer the black king and queen. It gives check. The king must move out of check. This leaves the queen to be taken.

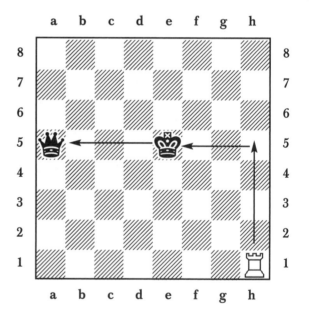

Here, you can see the king has moved out of check. The rook can now take the black queen.

Here is a skewer by a bishop. Again the king is in check.

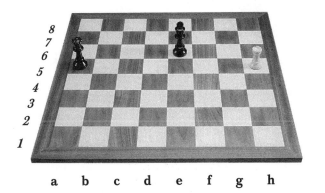

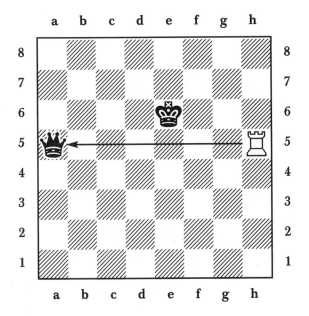

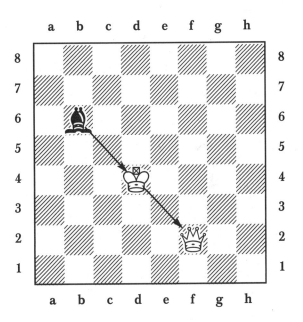

When the king moves, it will leave the white queen at the bishop's mercy.

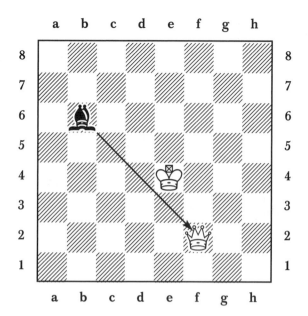

Kasparov Skewer and Discovered Attack

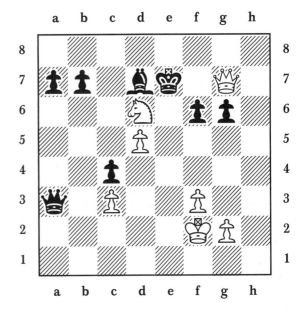

It's not often that we see a skewer and a discovered attack opportunity in the space of a few moves, but World Champion Garry Kasparov had that chance in this game from the 1986 Chess Olympiad in Dubai (UAE).

First, the skewer.

Here, at right, White's queen at **g7** has Black's king in check. Notice that the black king could take the white knight. What happens *if* it does?

---

1 .....   Ke7 × d6

Do you see? With his move, White can play a skewer in this position.

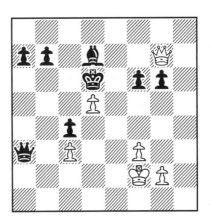

2 Qg7 – f8+

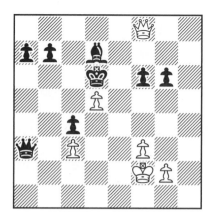

Black's king must now move out of check. The diagonal will now be clear for the white queen to travel along it and take the black queen.

Stefano Tatai spots the danger of this skewer, so *instead* he plays...

1 ..... Ke7 – d8

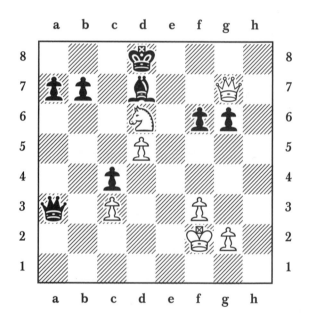

2 Qg7 – f8+

Kasparov replies with a check.

At the same time, Kasparov is still looking at the position of the black queen. If he can move the knight, he has a chance of discovered attack. He waits to see what Tatai will play.

What do you think Tatai should do?

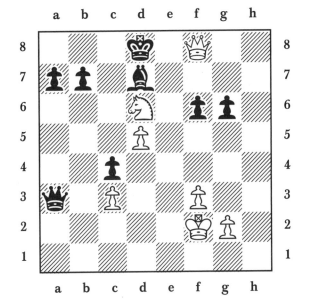

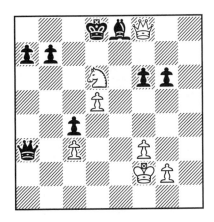

If Tatai blocks with the bishop, White's queen takes it with check and then the king is forced to move to **c7**. In order to avoid this, Tatai has no choice but to move his king to **c7**.

2 .....   Kd8 – c7

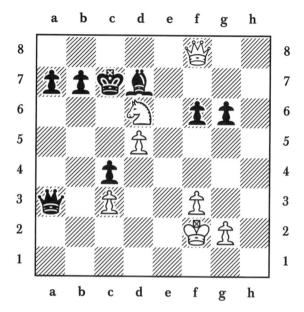

3 Nd6 – b5+

Black must avoid the check either by moving the king or by taking the knight.

The way is now free for Kasparov's queen to take Black's queen. Neatly done by the world champion!

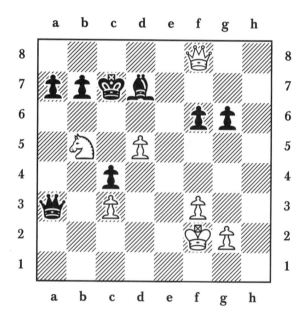

TEST YOUR PROGRESS: SKEWER

Here are another six positions for you to solve. As usual what you have learned in this chapter will help you to find the answers. First of all, try them without using a board. Then set the position up and see if you can work it out without touching any of the pieces.

(Answers on page 122)

1. Black to move
A check lets Black make a skewer.

2. Black to move
Can you find a skewer here?

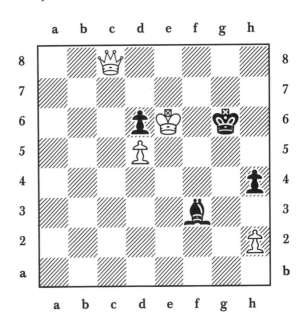

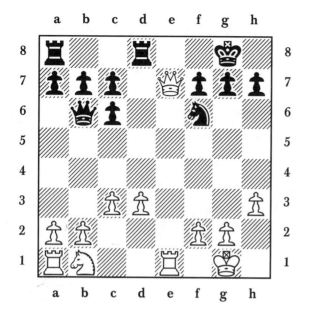

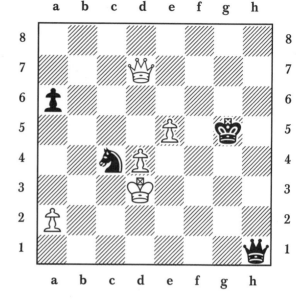

3. Black to move
Can you see how attacking the queen wins a piece?

4. Black to move
A check leads to a winning skewer.

5. Black to move
A knight fork leads to a winning skewer.

6. White to move
White's pawn looks to be in trouble. How does White win?

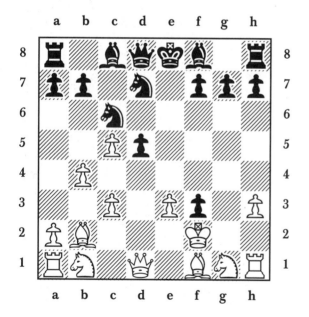

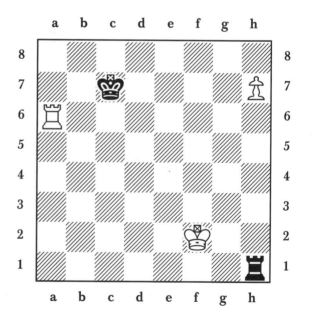

PART SEVEN
A MATING RACE

King and Two Bishops Vs. King

God save his Majesty!

Shakespeare—*Henry VI Part 2*

Next, on the following pages we'll show you an important ending...one that *forces* checkmate. It is definitely one for you to try. Watch the movement of the pieces closely, and then see if you can do it, too.

Before we do that, it ought to be pointed out, however, that while a king and two bishops can *force* a checkmate, a king and two knights—as shown at right—can- not. Sure, what we have here *is* check- mate, but the black king could easily have avoided it...by simply staying away from the corner!

Before we start, let's show you what we are trying to do.

This is one possibility:

Here is another example:

Look closely at these two boards and note where the pieces are positioned.

The idea to keep in mind for the first "trap" is that you want to drive the black king toward a corner. Two knights can't force his majesty into the corner of the board, but two bishops *can*.

Let's start here and see how the bishops imprison the king.

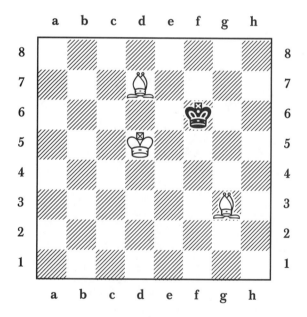

WINNING CHESS TACTICS & STRATEGIES

1 Bg3 – h4+

This is check. The king is forced to retreat.

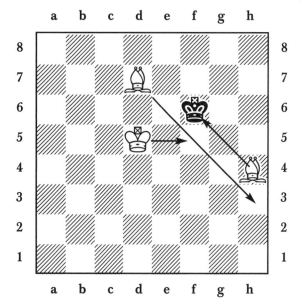

1 .....   Kf6 – g6

It's rather like a road block set up by the two bishops. There's no crossing the lines.

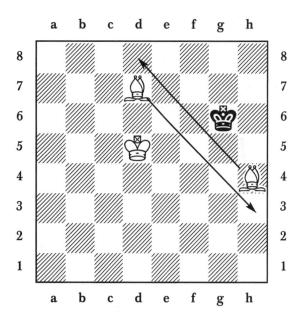

2 Kd5 – e5

You need your king to help with the finish.

2 .....   Kg6 – f7

The black king paces around inside his pen of
nine squares.

3 Ke5 – f5

The white king now takes away one of the nine
squares. Where does Black go now? Yes, to **g7**.

3 .....   Kf7 – g7

He tries to stay out of the corner.

4 Bd7 – e8

White seizes another diagonal. The roadblock has moved forward and the net is closing in. Black's king is now limited to six squares in the corner.

4 .....   Kg7 – f8

The king strikes at this bishop. He tries a break-out!

5 Be8 – g6

Now the black king is down to just five squares.

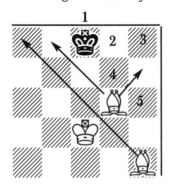

5 .....   Kf8 – g7

He stays out of the corner as long as possible.

6 Bh4 – e7

Black's "pen" has shrunk to four squares. Which square do you think the black king should move to now—**h6**? **g8**? **h8**? Think. Which is best?

No, not **h6**!

If Black does, the white bishop's following move, from **e7**, would give checkmate at…**f8**.

Does the position look familiar? Remember our second example on page 72?

Instead…

6 .....   Kg7 – g8

This is best. Stay out of the corner.

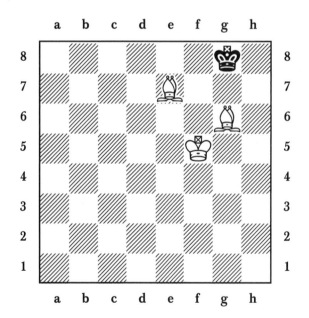

7 Kf5 – f6

The net closes. Black now has only two squares
—**g8** and **h8**.

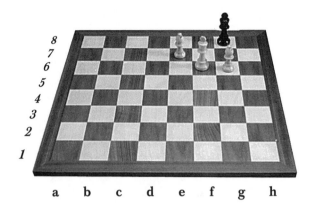

7 .....   g8 – h8

It's the only move. He can now move on only
two squares. But be careful! Don't make the mistake of cutting the black king's space down to
one square. Why?

For you to win, your opponent's king must be
in check. If, as shown below, the king has no safe
place to go, but it is not actually in check, play
is stalemated—neither side can win. (Your opponent has *avoided losing!*)

Look here at this partial board. Note what
happens if white should mistakenly move **f6 –
f7?**. (In notation, the "?" means this is *not* a good
move.)

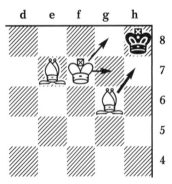

A stalemated game is a draw, so you only get
half a point. Naturally, you prefer to win, and
gain the full game point, so…

To continue the mating race, now we just
need to bring in the white king. It will take two
moves to get the pieces into position. Let's finish
up the mating race. We'll show you the rest on
partial boards.

8 Bg6 – f5

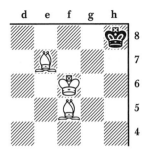

The bishop makes way for the white king to get to **g6**. The bishops need him to cover **h7** to get the mate.

8 ..... Kh8 – g8

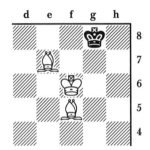

The black king still has two squares only. It's a good thing he has two. Otherwise it would be stalemate.

9 f6 – g6

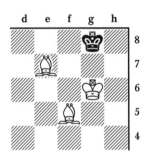

Now the king takes over **g6** and controls **h7**, **g7**, and **f7**. He can now help deliver the mate.

9 ..... Kg8 – h8

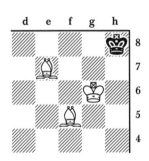

Be careful. A bishop move from **f5** to **e6** will be stalemate! Be patient.

10 Be7 – d6

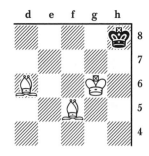

Waiting only.

10 ..... Kg8 – h8

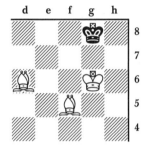

No choice.

11 Bf5 – e6+

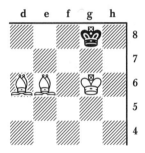

Now, in for the final moves to checkmate.

11 ..... Kg8 – h8

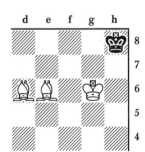

Nearly there. Do you see it coming?

12 **Bd6 – e5** checkmate

The bishop on the dark square (dark bishop) gives checkmate. The king helps by covering the only square that the bishops cannot reach.

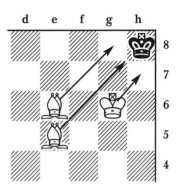

A PAIR OF RACES

Now, here are two mating races to try. In both races, Black moves first. Count only his moves.

In the one below, how many moves do you need as Black to give checkmate? We took just five. (Playing as White, you will make it harder for Black if you try to attack one of the rooks.)

Now try the race below. Because the queen is a stronger piece than the rook, the win as Black should be easier. In fact, it should take only four moves.

In your play, however, remember to stay alert, and beware of stalemate!

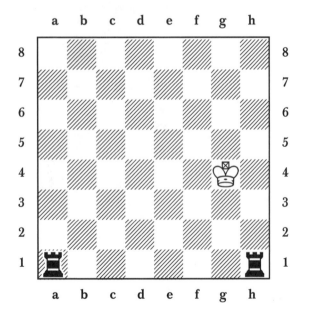

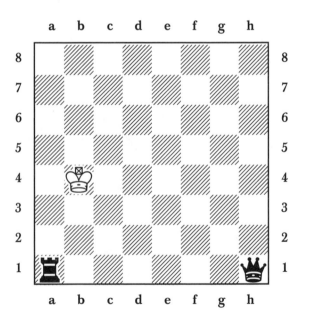

PART EIGHT

IMPROVING PIECE PLAY

Advantage is a better soldier than rashness!

Shakespeare—*Henry V*

It's vital in any sport to get into the best play position. Recently, a horse won an important race in the last few yards. Throughout the race, the rider kept his horse just behind the leaders, ready to strike for home. The jockey knew if he went too soon, his horse might falter because he was energized by "the chase." If the horse was moved ahead too soon it might slow; too late and there would be no time to catch up. The rider timed it perfectly. And won! Like that jockey, you have to time things well. But you also need to plan, and arrange to be in your best position to strike and win.

Look again at "A Dream Start" (pages 12–13). The game's begun. Now you need a plan for the rest of the game. In chess, it's vital to arrange for open lines for your pieces. Before each of your moves, gradually learn to ask yourself the five following questions to help decide what to do and cut down on mistakes:

1. What is my opponent trying to do?
2. Does it affect my plan?
3. What do I do next?
4. Is there an even better move than that one?
5. Do I understand the position better now?

The Bishop

Let's examine here how the player with the black pieces manages to extend the range of his bishop.

Try following the moves, and if you have trouble you can set it up on your board.

1 d2 – d4   the Queen's Pawn opening

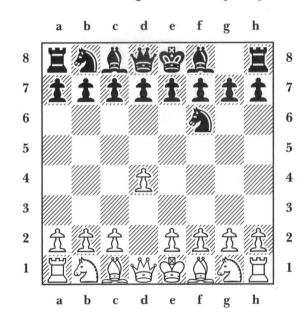

1 .....   **Ng8 – f6**

This move stops White from playing **e2 – e4**.

2 c2 – c4   g7 – g6

So the white pawn attacks the center and Black prepares to put the bishop on **g7** and on the long diagonal **h8 – a1**.

3 Nb1 – c3   d7 – d5

White again attacks the center, and Black challenges there.

4 Bc1 – f4   Bf8 – g7

Black's bishop is on the diagonal **h8 – a1**, the line of squares along which he can best strike into the heart of the enemy.

5 e2 – e3   0 – 0

This white pawn supports the one on **d4**. Black castles to safety and brings a rook into play.

6 Ng1 – f3   c7 – c5

Black is not satisfied with the number of squares his bishop on **g7** can move to. He wants to break up the center to give his king's bishop a clear path.

7 d4 × c5   Qd8 – a5

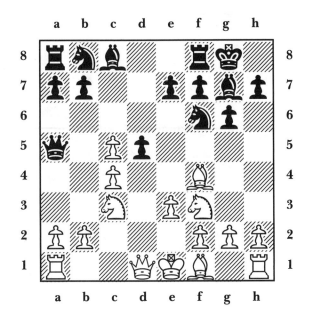

Black now brings in the queen to cooperate.

8 c4 × d5

White's move is suicide! His king is still vulnerable in the center. He needs to keep the lines *closed* until his king is safe.

8 .....   Nf6 × d5

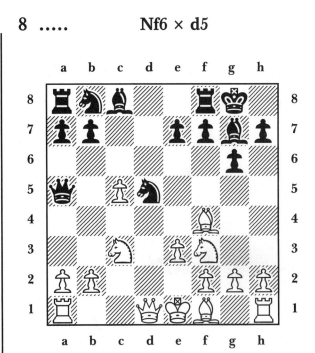

This last move opens the lines for the bishop to strike. Three black pieces are now bearing down on the white knight at **c3**.

9 Qd1 × d5   a rash move

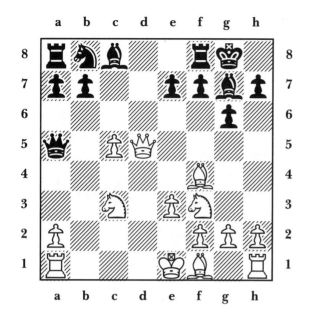

10 b2 × c3   Qa5 × c3+

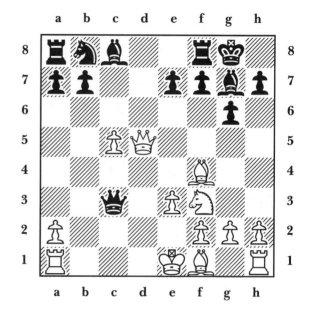

White now loses the rook at **a1**.

9 .....   Bg7 × c3+

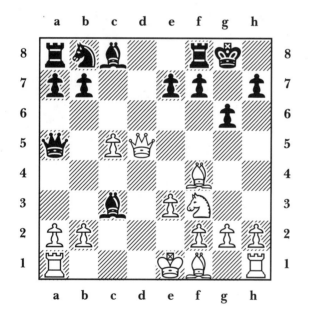

The bishop's capture of the rook leads to disaster.

There *is* something more to say about bishops. Have you noticed that, on a chess board, your two bishops never meet; that is, land on the same square? Have you noticed why? What colors are their squares?

A lesson learned: When your king is vulnerable in the middle of the board, *always* keep the central lines *closed*!

BISHOPS OF OPPOSITE COLORS

Bishops of opposite colors in an endgame is often a draw.

In the diagram below, White's bishop has no power to exert because the black king is on a white square. This white bishop cannot move off the black squares.

Black's bishop, on the other hand, will move endlessly along the diagonal **f7 – a2** or other white squares. He cannot move to black squares. The game is a draw.

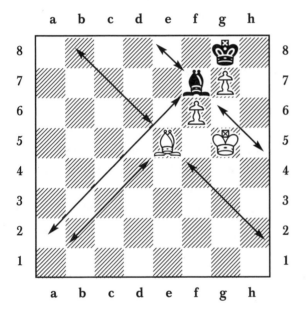

However, when there are other powerful pieces on the board the presence of opposite-colored bishops can be a definite advantage because one of the opposite-colored bishops may be unable to defend a square attacked by the other.

The Rooks

The rooks are the "Batman and Robin" of the chess board. Look at the diagram below. Where is it you want the rooks to be?

Along the seventh rank, because there they would be able to strike at Black's pawns.

How do you get them there? Is anything stopping you? Take a good look, then turn the page to see how you would make your way into position.

1 Bg5 – e7

This bishop/rook fork forces a take. Move the rook and Black loses the bishop. Move the bishop, the rook is lost for a bishop—a very poor trade.

1 ..... Bd6 × e7

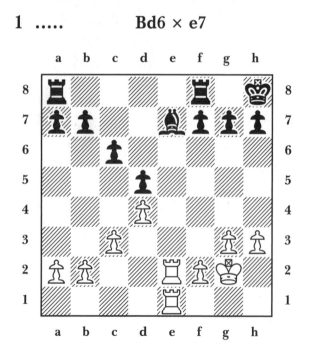

2 Re2 × e7 Ra8 – b8

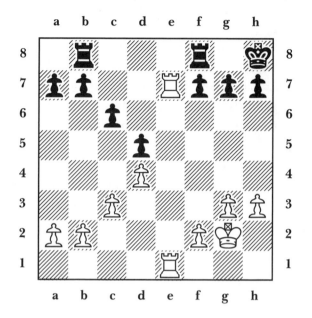

After White's move, the white rook has arrived and is in position to take the **b7** pawn. Black moves, but is in trouble.

White can now double his rooks (Batman and Robinlike), along the seventh rank with **Re7 – d7**. Then, except at the cost of several pawns, Black can't stop him from following up with the other rook to the seventh rank, **Re1 – e7**. After that, Black's pawns will start to fall in earnest.

The Queen

The queen and the rook are sometimes called the "heavy pieces." They're so powerful that they are like big cannons. They can inflict great damage on the enemy forces, but need to be positioned correctly, so they can exert their great powers over the board effectively.

The most powerful attacking piece, the queen, moves like both a bishop and a rook. Imagining it at the center of the board, you can see its power shooting from it like lasers! Of the 64 squares on the chess board at right, how many do you count that are under the queen's control?

The queen shouldn't be brought out too early, rarely alone, and not left exposed (or open) to attacks from less valuable pieces. Normally, a queen should not be placed in the center of the board early in the game.

As the game goes on, rows or diagonals will become open, unblocked by other pieces and pawns. Such open routes are perfect for the queen, because of her long-range power!

Later in the game, it is ideal for the queen, as well as the rook, to penetrate into your opponent's position, so that all of her great force pushes against the enemy position.

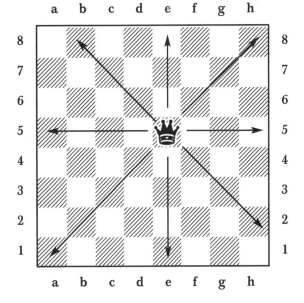

The queen and its reach look like an octopus!

Photo by Jami L. Anson, courtesy U.S. Chess Federation, New Windsor, NY 12553

Queen Moves

Look at the position at right. If the white queen takes the rook on **a8**, then the black queen will take the white bishop on **e5** and Black will certainly be in no danger of losing the game.

But White's queen does have the whole h1 – a8 diagonal to travel freely on.

So, what to do?

What follows is a little "in-between" move—experts use the German word "zwischenzug."

Instead of going for the rook, White heads in the opposite direction with **Qd5 – f3+** (below).

The **Qd5 – f3+** move forces the black king onto the back row at either **g8** or **e8**. The white queen will then take the black rook, and check. After the check, White will be able to save the bishop.

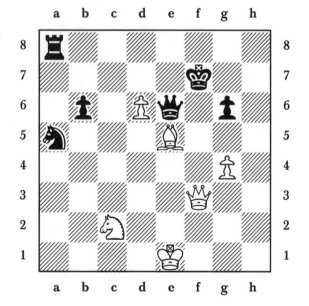

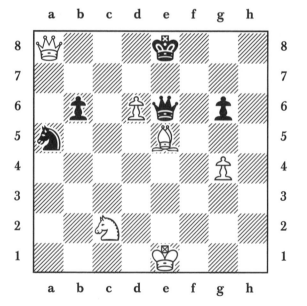

The Knight

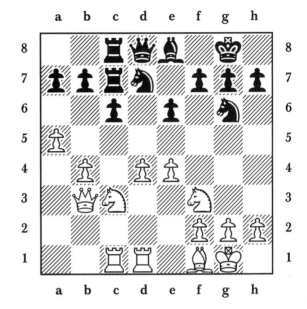

Like the other pieces, the knight enjoys being in the middle of the board, where there are more choices available for a good move. Unlike the other pieces, he is quite happy in a crowd. After all, he can easily leave by jumping right over the top when he wants out!

Putting these two ideas together, you can see that the knight is also able to strike quickly into the heart of enemy territory. With your knight, you don't have to wait for an enemy to leave lines open before your pieces can attack.

KNIGHT PLAY

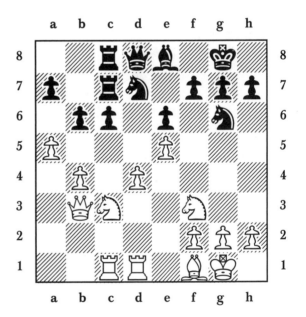

Let's see a fine example of knight play. In 1921, Capablanca at last had the opportunity to play the world champion Emanuel Lasker for the title. In the eleventh game of the match—which Capablanca won with four wins, no losses, and ten draws—both Capablanca and Lasker moved their knights to formidable outposts. It is quite instructive to watch them do it.

We start with the position top right, and it's White's play.

WHITE   **BLACK**
Capablanca   Lasker

20 e4 – e5   **b7 – b6**

Capablanca now has a post at **d6** for his knight, and Black replies with a pawn move.

21 Nc3 – e4   Rc8 – b8

This white knight is ready to go to its outpost at
d6. Black responds with a rook move.

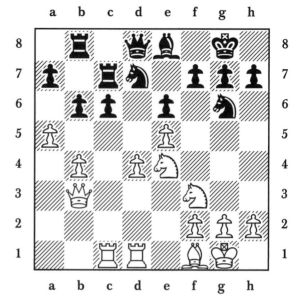

22 Qb3 – c3

This move gets the queen off the line of the
black rook, but loses time because now Lasker
sees a good outpost for his knight at **d5.**

22 .....   Ng6 – f4

Black is preparing to go to **d5** to attack the
queen.

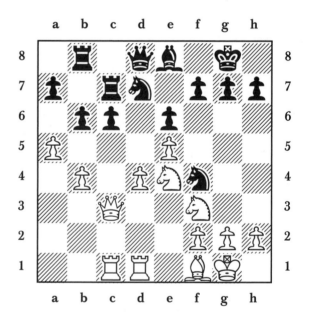

23 Ne4 – d6

Now Capablanca's knight comes to an excellent outpost.

23 .....   Nf4 – d5

Lasker's knight also comes to an excellent outpost, attacking the white queen!

Do you see how both players have improved their knights to wonderful positions? Can you look ahead in your games and do this, too? (Capablanca eventually won the game on his 48th move.)

The King

In the position at right, the black rooks are tying down all White's pieces. Capablanca is playing Black against Boris Kostich.

Capablanca examines the position to find how he can improve his pieces and pile on the pressure. Amazingly, he looks at the king. It's just sitting there—not doing much of anything! He thinks, *I can trade the rooks and minor pieces whenever I wish. Where do I want my king? At far away b3!* He plays...

51 ..... Kf7 – e7

See the effect of this move in the diagram at right below.

As usual, Capablanca played perfectly!

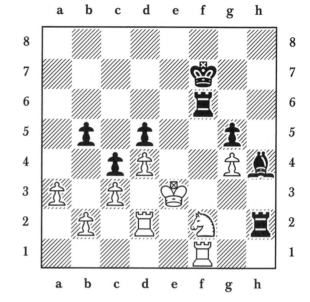

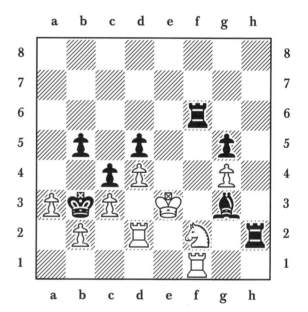

J. R. Capablanca and wife, Olga

Photo courtesy of www.chesscafe.com

PART NINE

THE ENDGAME

Harry Pillsbury, an American Master

O What a noble mind is here o'erthrown
The courtiers, soldiers, scholar's eye, tongue, sword
The expectancy and rose of the fair state
The glass of fashion and the mould of form
                    Shakespeare—*Hamlet*

England's famed Prime Minister Winston Churchill is reputed to have had a good memory. For his headmaster, it was said that he learned twelve hundred lines of Macaulay's *Lays of Ancient Rome* without a single mistake.

Well, Churchill's memory was good, but the chances are that Harry Nelson Pillsbury had, if not a better one, at least one as good. As good-looking as a Hollywood film star, a Redford or a Gere, this tall, easygoing American from Somerville, Massachusetts, was a legend in his time.

One day in London, before Pillsbury gave his usual exhibition of twenty *simultaneous* blind-fold-chess games and a game of whist, two professors came to him. They had chosen a list of thirty-two words or phrases designed to test and perhaps defeat Pillsbury's noted memory. Their list consisted of the following:

antiphlogistine - periosteum - takadiastase - plasmon - threlkeld - streptococcus - staphylococcus - mirococcus - plasmodium - Mississippi - Freiheit - Philadelphia - Cincinnati - athletics - no war - Echtenerg - American - Russian - philosophy - Piet Potgleter's Rost - Salamagundi - Domisillecootsi - Banginanvate - Schlecter's Neck - Manzinyama - theosophy - catechism - Madjesoomalops

Pillsbury took the paper, quickly studied the words, and passed the list back. Then he recited the whole list forwards...*and backwards.* The professors left, no doubt stunned, while Pillsbury went on with his exhibition. The following day, Pillsbury repeated the word list *again.*

Most everyone who is very good at playing chess seems to have learned how at a very young age. Paul Morphy was eight, Wilhelm Steinitz was twelve, Emanuel Lasker ten, José Capablanca four, Alexander Alekhine eleven, Max Euwe four, Mikhail Botvinnik twelve, Vassily Smyslov six, Milhal Tal eight, Tigran Petrosian eight, Boris Spassky five, Robert Fischer six—and this is a list of the world champions. Pillsbury learned to play at the age of sixteen; late by anybody's standards. As soon as his talent was recognized, he moved to New York

City and settled in at the Brooklyn Chess Club. Three years later, he was ranked as the strongest player in America. In 1895, the Hastings Chess Club in England invited the world's best players to its tournament, and Pillsbury was included. Later, when Pillsbury returned to America, he told journalists he had expected to finish in the first three, but that's all. He did better than that. He was a clear winner. At twenty-three, he was only marginally older than Paul Morphy when Morphy had beaten the world's best. Pillsbury's victory was no fluke, for his style was bold and energetic—typically American. It was clear to all at Hastings that here was a great new player.

But Pillsbury's story is a sad one—and world champion he was not to be. Later that year, he traveled to St. Petersburg, Russia, and there contracted a disease that was to kill him. The world champion, Emanuel Lasker, was deeply moved by his death, saying, "Those who knew Pillsbury in the days of his early youth will never forget the striking, almost beautiful face which he bore in those days." Lasker went on to lament that Pillsbury, "gifted with pleasant and lovable traits," had to spend so much time doing exhibitions of blindfold chess and memory displays, and it was that, in Lasker's opinion, which had killed him.

What a great pity and tragedy that Pillsbury, perhaps one of the greatest tournament players of all time, was struck down at the height of his powers. The poet Keats wrote, "the good die young." This was Pillsbury's fate. Who knows but if he had not died at such an early age, he might well have become the best chess player of all time. Certainly, he was an American phenomenon.

Pillsbury Plays the Endgame

On Pillsbury's return to America, after his victory at Hastings, he was given a banquet in Brooklyn, New York. Specially done up on the cover of the menus were positions from his games. One of the games chosen was one he played against Isidor Gunsberg.

Pillsbury plays White in this fascinating endgame. In the position below, he has a "passed" pawn, a pawn unopposed by enemy pawns, on the "c" line. His opponent, Gunsberg, as Black, has chances with his outside pawns on the "a" and "b" lines.

Gunsberg, Pillsbury's opponent, earned fame in chess as the player behind Mephisto, the chess robot that toured Europe fooling kings and commoners alike. Gunsberg worked the "robot" from inside of it. Even Napoleon, in a slightly earlier time, was fooled by it. In the guise of Mephisto, Gunsberg won an English Counties Championship in 1878. Gunsburg, as himself, was a contender for the World Championship in 1890.

Now let's look at this endgame.

WHITE	BLACK
Pillsbury	Gunsberg

1 f4 – f5

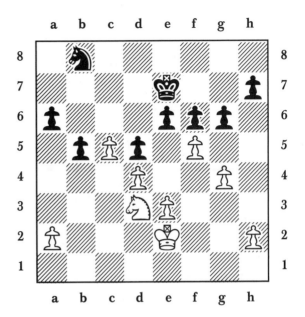

Pillsbury wants to bring his knight to **f4** to attack the pawn on **d5**. If Gunsberg captures **f5**, he will loosen the defenses of the pawn on **d5**. He chooses another way.

1 .....   g6 – g5

Gunsberg stops the knight from going to **f5**.

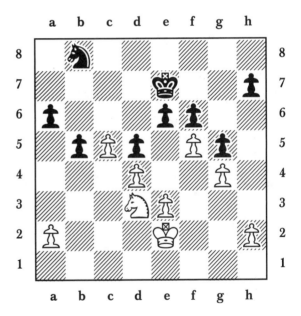

2 Ne3 – b4

Pillsbury brings his knight another way to attack the pawn on **d5**. It is also supporting a possible advance of his passed pawn to **c6**.

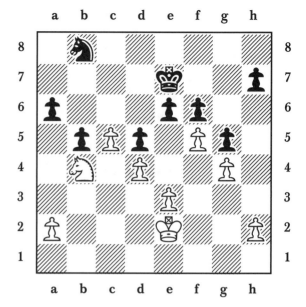

2 .....   a6 – a5

Gunsberg decides to drive the knight away. He must do something!

3 c5 – c6

The pawn advances anyway. If Gunsburg takes
the knight, then Pillsbury will push his pawn
again, and it cannot be stopped from promotion
to a queen.

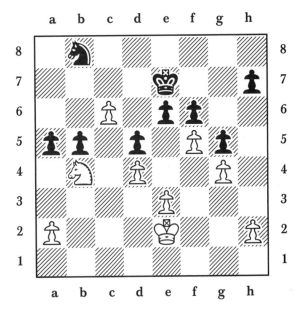

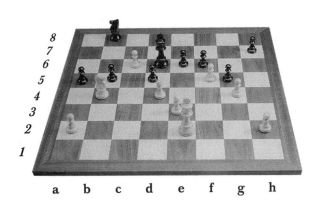

3 .....   Ke7 – d6

The king has to do sentry duty.

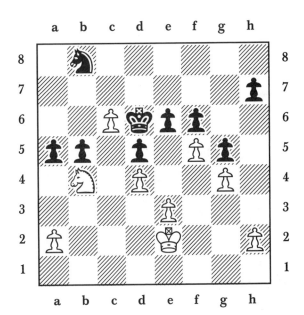

4   f5 × e6

Now there are two passed pawns for Gunsburg's king to patrol. If he takes the knight now, then the pawn on **e6** advances. The king must then take it, leaving the pawn on **c6** to sail through to **c7,** where it attacks the knight on **b8**. If the knight moves, the pawn goes to **c8** to queen and the king cannot stop it.

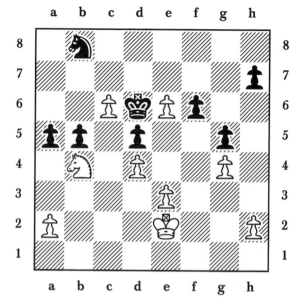

4   .....   Nb8 × c6

Gunsburg must stop these dangerous pawns. He captures one with his knight. Will it be enough?

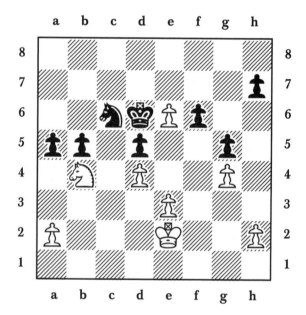

5 Nb4 × Nc6

Pillsbury trades knights. Now he gambles every-
thing on his pawn on **e6**. Just see how he gets
support to it.

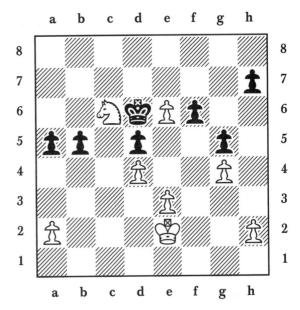

5 ..... K × c6

The king recaptures. If only now he can quickly
get across to **e6** and take the advanced pawn…

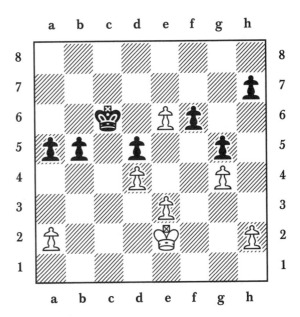

6 e3 – e4

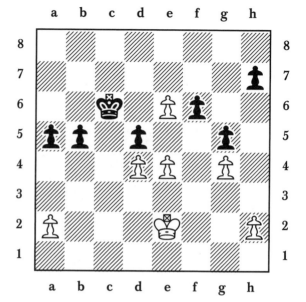

This is how Pillsbury gets support to the advanced pawn. This technique very important to learn.

Pillsbury aims for this position. If two pawns are together like this, the king cannot take the back one because the other will leap forward and cannot be caught.

6 .....   d5 × e4

Gunsberg has really no choice but to take this pawn. Now you can see Pillsbury's plan.

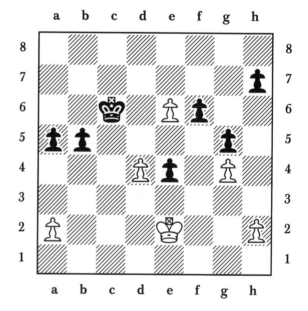

7 d4 – d5+

Now Pillsbury brings up support. Black's king is tied to patrolling these dangerous pawns. He cannot take them.

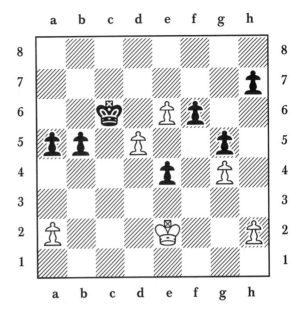

7 .....   Kc6 – d6

The king tucks in on sentry duty; however, this is not good. This king is chained, he has to prevent the king's pawn from promoting to queen. Meanwhile, Pillsbury's king is free to wander all over the board.

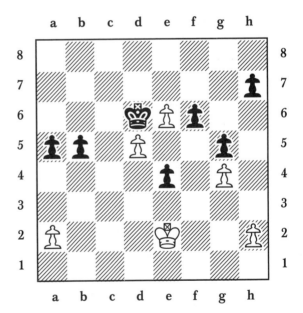

8 Ke2 – e3

Pillsbury's king advances to mop up the black pawn on **e4**.

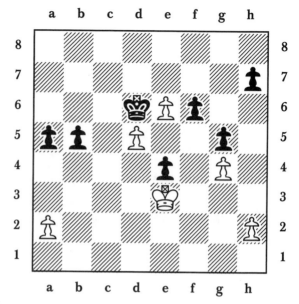

8 .....   b5 – b4

Gunsberg's outside pawns rush on. They are dangerous, and Pillsbury's king will have to watch them. At least he has a king that can do so.

9 Ke3 × e4

Pillsbury has time to mop up this pawn and still look after the dangerous outside ones. How many moves does it take Pillsbury's king now to go to **a1**?

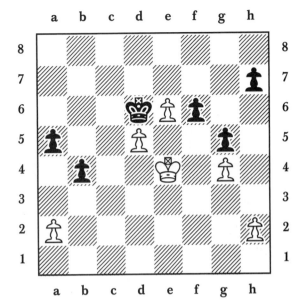

9 .....   a5 – a4

Gunsberg is forcing Pillsbury's king to the "a" and "b" lines.

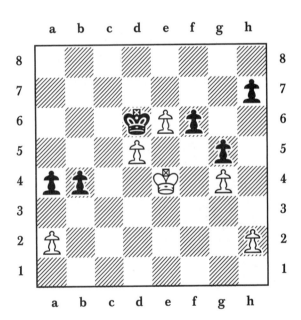

10 Ke4 – d4

Pillsbury's king comes over to **d4** to stop any breakthrough.

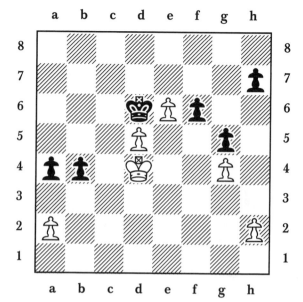

10 .....   h7 – h5

Gunsberg's king is holed up in the center. His pawns on the "a" and "b" lines are patrolled by Pillsbury's king. What is left? Attack on the other wing.

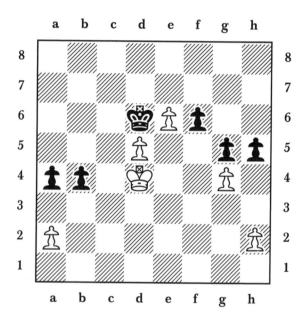

11   g4 × h5

This seems to have given Pillsbury an outside passed pawn with just three squares to go.

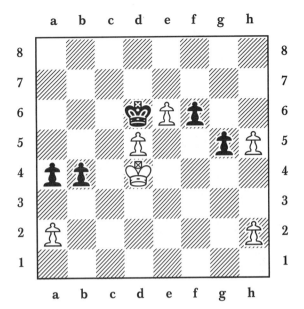

11   .....   a4 – a3

Gunsberg makes a last throw of the dice. He has a plan.

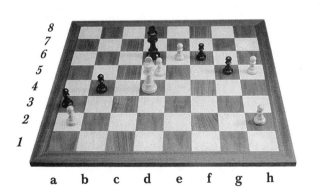

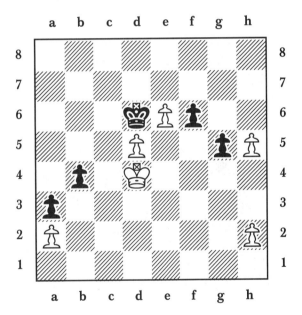

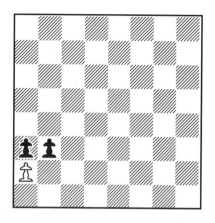

Look at this. It's important for you to learn this endgame trick. Black's plan is to get into this position…

…and then, after White's next move, **a2 × b3**, his "a" pawn is free to promote to a queen.

But Pillsbury won't let him follow that plan.

12 Kd4 – c4

Pillsbury's king comes across and puts a stop to it.

12 .....   f6 – f5

This is much too slow.

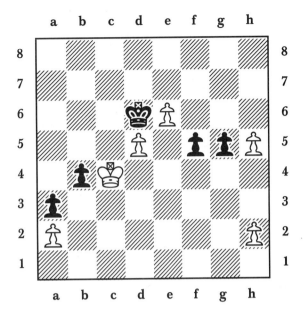

13 h5 – h6

Isidor Gunsberg now resigns. Pillsbury's pawn will queen and easily mop up Gunsberg's "f" and "g" pawns.

Pillsbury's play in this endgame is perfect. If you play it through, you'll learn a lot about what it takes to be a master of the endgame like Pillsbury.

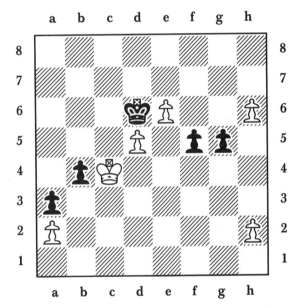

 DID YOU KNOW?

André Philidor, the great French chess player of the 1700s, was also a noted composer of French operas. He believed that "Pawns are the soul of chess!" and he was right. Keeping pawns "healthy" is a large part of a winning game plan, so be sure to check out and study the back of the book Strategy Tips. Commit the pawn and other chess "rules" of strategy to memory, and you'll be glad you did.

Abe Yanofsky, a Canadian Prodigy

Because the family was Jewish, the Yanofskys left their home in Russia in 1925. Daniel Abraham Yanofsky was born in Brody, Poland, as the family passed through that country on the way to Canada. His Canadian schoolmates soon took to calling him "Abe," after the great United States President Abraham Lincoln.

At the age of eight, young Abe saw a chess set in a shop window and persuaded his father to buy it and teach him the game. He joined the Winnipeg Chess Club, but rapidly became too good to play anyone there, so he was sent to Toronto to play in tournaments.

In Toronto one Saturday, he signed up for three tournaments: the "under 12s" in the morning, "under 18s" in the afternoon, and "adult major" in the evening. After a single U-12 game, it was immediately apparent that he was too good for that age group. The organizers asked him to withdraw from that section, which he did—but he went on to win easily both the other championships.

At the age of fourteen, Abe played board two for Canada at the Buenos Aires Olympiad, where he scored 84.4 percent, a sensational result. Alexander Alekhine, the world champion at the time, spent hours with young Abe, going over the boy's games.

Unfortunately, the year was 1939, and it spelled the end of Abe's budding friendship with Alekhine, who was forced back to Nazi Germany to be with his wife. The war also caused the suspension of chess tournaments around the world. Although the world situation did not stop Abe from becoming a chess grandmaster, it probably prevented him from reaching his full potential.

After World War II ended, Abe was able to do other things besides play chess. In 1952, the Canadian Bar Association awarded him a scholarship as the most outstanding law student in Canada. But his youthful chess record is still to be admired. For your enjoyment and enlightenment, here is one of his games.

At Fourteen, Abe's Tight Corner

Fourteen-year-old Abe Yanofsky was playing for his adopted country, Canada, in the 1939 Olympiad when he was faced with this problem. Playing White in this position, if Abe moves his attacked queen off the g-file, Black mates by…

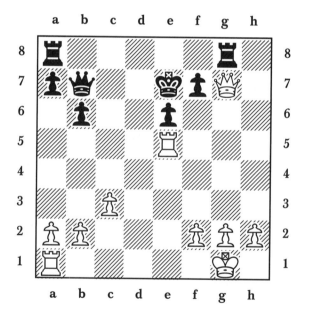

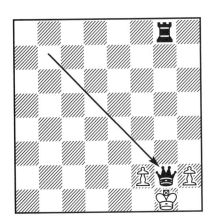

..... Qb7 × g2

Oh, oh, can't
have that!

But Abe searched for an answer and found it.

1 Re5 × e6+

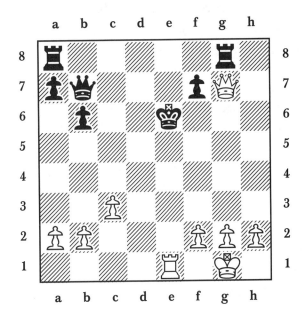

Black's f-pawn was pinned and could not take,
so White's move drove the black king into the
open.

1 .....   Ke7 × e6

Now White brought his *other* rook to the attack.

2 Ra1 – e1+

Black sidestepped.

2 .....   **Ke6 – d6**

White played…

3 Qg7 – f6+

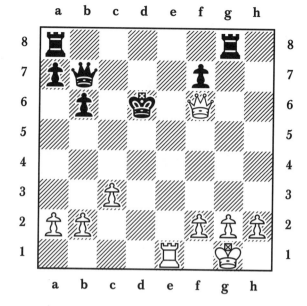

Notice now that *if* Abe's opponent had next played **3. ..... Kd6 – d7**, White's **4. Re1 – e7+** would have attacked the black king and queen on the same line. Do you remember that such an attack is called a "skewer"? Black would have lost his queen for the white rook.

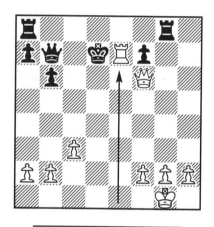

Black, still hoping to escape, played…

3 .....   **Kd6 – d5**

But White continued his attack.

4 Re1 – e5+

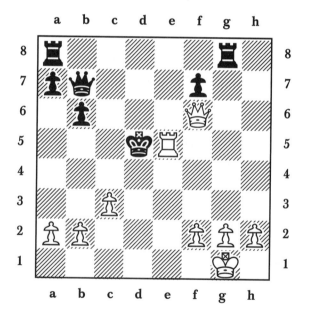

Black was forced to play...

4 .....   Kd5 – c4

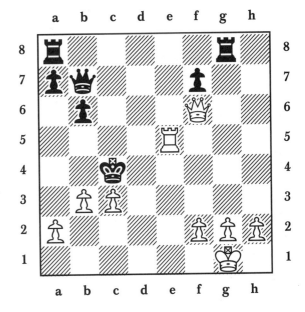

Abe now used his pawn.

5 b2 – b3+

5 .....   Kc4 – d3

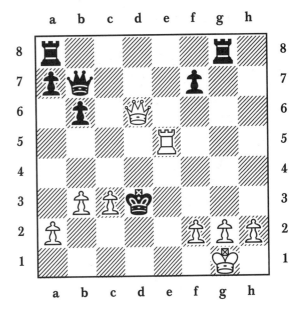

The black king is really on the run now, and moving into White's camp!

6 Qf6 – d6+

White gives chase.

6 .....   **Kd3 – c2**

The black king is heading for Abe's base line.

7 Re5 – e2+

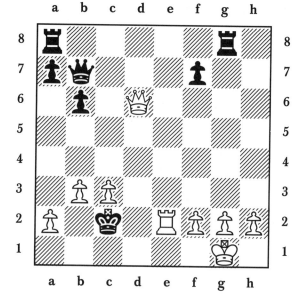

7 .....   **Kc2 – c1**

He's arrived on the base line…

8 Qd6 – d2+

…the white queen on his tail.

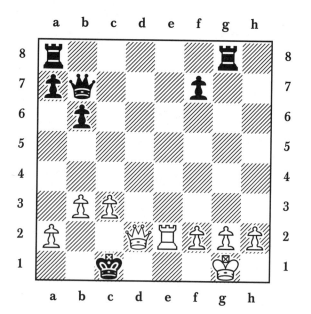

8 .....   Kc1 – b1

He could have resigned long ago.

9 Qd2 – d1 checkmate

And look...Black is *still* waiting to give check-mate on **g2**! No wonder the world champion Alekhine spent hours with the fourteen-year-old Yanofsky!

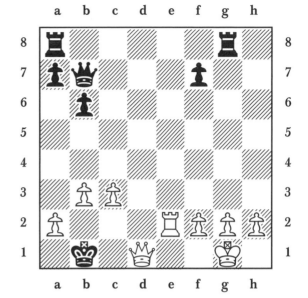

PART TEN

A GAME TO END ALL

Rudolf Charousek

This story shall the good man teach his son
Shakespeare—*King Henry V*

When one of your authors was a boy, he used to scan the names of unraced two-year-olds, trying to pick a Derby winner. The Aga Khan owned strings of horses with strange-sounding names—Rustam, Blenheim, Migoli, Firdaussi—all with very good lines. One year, looking through the list of horses, he saw a name that filled him with excitement: "Dust Devil."

Well, this horse never ran as a two-year-old. The boy looked for the horse's name all the next year, in every racing paper his father took. Finally, there it was! Dust Devil was listed to run in the final classic race of the year, the Doncaster St. Leger. Full of "Dust Devil," the boy told everyone he knew to back it. No one but an uncle succumbed to the sage advice, and he backed it to win only. Dust Devil came in second. The boy was thrilled; his uncle not so, because he had lost his money. But a horse the boy had picked had become thrillingly real.

How does this tale relate to chess? Very much like when the boy had first spotted the name Dust Devil, he once came upon the name of Charousek at school while doing research in the *Encyclopaedia Britannica*. Charousek… Charousek …a name to roll around on your tongue.

Rudolf Charousek: born 1873, died 1900. He was only twenty-seven years old when he died. Twenty-seven! It made you think of all those great English poets who had died when they were very young. How had this young student appeared in the lists of the very great?

In scouring chess books, books with collections of great games at the local library, the boy finally spotted a remark that Emanuel Lasker made after the Nuremberg, Germany, Tournament of 1896. Lasker became world champion that year and was to stay world champion until the year 1921. He was a good champion. It's been said often that, if ever there was a time machine to take the great players of today back to yesteryear to play the great players then, one champion they would *not* relish playing would be Lasker. Nobody won so many apparently lost games as Lasker did.

Lasker won that tournament in Nuremberg in 1896 and then, after his game in the tournament with Charousek, said, "Someday I'll have to play this young man for the championship of the world." Looking to see where Charousek finished in the tournament, the boy was disappointed to find that Charousek had finished twelfth. Only twelfth! But then he looked further, to see who played whom in the tournament. One of the people that Charousek beat was Lasker.

Lasker's remark was a great compliment. Was it deserved? Sometimes people who die as young as Charousek did do not leave much information about themselves. We know a lot about John Keats, the young English poet who died at a similarly young age, because he wrote many letters to people, and there are, of course, also his poems. John Keats' letters tell us a lot about his attitude toward life, and also about the girl he loved, Fanny Brawne.

Charousek has this same "Keatsian" quality. We know from his games he was brilliant. And we know he was not very rich. When he was a student at the University of Prague, he very much wanted to own the great German chess classic, *The Handbook of Chess Openings.* Charousek could not afford to buy it, so he borrowed a copy from a friend and copied it out by hand, page by page, until he had his own copy of the chess openings.

Lasker's words after the Nuremberg tournament were astute if not prophetic. Nuremberg was Charousek's first international tournament and, although he finished only twelfth, a few weeks later he tied for first place with Chigorin in an international tournament in Budapest.

And who was Chigorin? He never became a world champion, it is true, but he had played Lasker for the title. Mikhail Chigorin was, at that time, already one of the super "grandmasters," although the term did not then yet exist. What is important is that this Russian, who lived in Czarist Russia, is now regarded as the most important influence on twentieth-century Russian chess.

All young Russian grandmasters come under the influence of Mikhail Chigorin. From him they have learned both the value of attack and the fighting spirit. The Russian school of chess, which has always been strong in world chess and almost totally dominant since World War II, owes its position to Chigorin, "the father of Russian chess," according to Mikhail Botvinnik, Russia's longest-serving world champion ever.

This, then, was the man that Charousek tied with at Budapest. It's true he was beaten three games to one in the playoff, but he was only twenty-three at the time and Chigorin was already a veteran master. Charousek's achievement was superb.

Charousek's early promise was fulfilled and confirmed a year later in Berlin, in 1897. This time, playing against a strong field, he finished first on his own. A year later, he won again on his own in Germany, and then again in Hungary. But now he was only two years away from the end of his life. The young man had fallen ill with tuberculosis, the great killer of his day, which had also destroyed the enormous poetic talent of the young Keats. For Charousek there was no hope. Medical science in those days had no cure for the disease. Charousek would not live to be a contender against Lasker for the world championship, but Lasker had indeed spotted a challenger —a "Dust Devil"—to watch out for.

We'll look now at a game played by Charousek in his old, romantic "Long Live Attack!" style. Of course, it doesn't reflect the twentieth-century approach to chess. The new century was just coming in as he died, but this beautiful game clearly shows him to be a master of combination.

A Dazzling Finish

Charousek learned to play chess in 1889 when he was sixteen. Only four years later, he sat down to play a game, noted now for its famous finish, against an opponent, J. Wollner, in the northern Hungarian city of Kassa. Who J. Wollner was, even whether his name was John or Joe or Jason, we don't know, for there is no further mention of him in chess history. But though he has vanished into the mists of time, the game he played one spring evening in 1893 has not.

It is only by the merest slice of good fortune that we have this game to give you, for it was not one played in a tournament. It's likely that some chess *aficionado,* sorting through Charousek's papers after he died, came across it and published it. Strangely, chess abounds with brilliant plays from friendly games: Paul Morphy's at the Paris Opera House and Adolf Anderssen's wonderful "Evergreen" and "Immortal" games played at the London café, "The Divan."

The great chess writer Ludek Pachman said "Strategy and tactics have much in common." Here you see Charousek using tactics like discovered checks, and doing all the sensible things we suggested you try to do, like bringing out pieces to the center, and using pieces as a team, all for one and one for all. This is strategy. You can't get your pieces to do wonderful things if you don't put them in position first. "Help your pieces to help you," said Paul Morphy.

Let us now drift back in time, to April 1893, where a young man knows that to be twenty is to be vibrantly alive. This is the spirit of Charousek's game, with the spring returned to Europe and the wars of the twentieth century far away.

WHITE	BLACK
Charousek	**Wollner**

1	e2 – e4	e7 – e5
2	d2 – d4	e5 × d4
3	c2 – c3	

This is the famous Danish Gambit. Today, with our systematic study of openings, there are lots of "gambits." A gambit is usually an offering of material, often a pawn, by White—who moves first—in order to speed up the transit of his pieces to the front line and find ways to use his tricks, like forks, skewers, and pins. It doesn't always work though. Gambits do not win every time.

3	.....	d4 × c3
4	Bf1 – c4	Ng8 – f6

Charousek swiftly brings a piece, his bishop, to attack the center, but today it's generally "knights before bishops."

5	Ng1 – f3	Bf8 – c5

Wollner has already proven one thing. He knows it's a fault to be greedy. He ignores capturing the pawn at **b2**.

6	Nb1 × c36	d7 – d6
7	0 – 0	0 – 0

Both players have had knights and bishops act appropriately and both have castled safely behind their wall of pawns. It can be a mistake to move pawns from in front of the castled king because enemy pieces can get in. Keep your king safe.

8 Nf3 – g5   h7 – h6

Wollner's move is weak. If his move had been **8. ..... Nb8–c6**, Wollner would have developed another piece and put more protection on central square **e5**. As it is, no piece is brought into play and the king's castled position is even slightly weakened. Playing through master games like this reveals the importance of the center. The next moves will continue to spotlight this.

9 Ng5 × f7   Rf8 × f7

White has sacrificed his knight for a mere pawn. He knows he should recover this material, so…

10 e4 – e5

Can you see why the black pawn on **d6** can't capture this invader? The queen on **d8** is in mortal danger, for the rook, in capturing Charousek's knight, is no longer defending the black queen.

10 .....   Nf6 – g4
11 e5 – e6

Charousek tries to recoup his lost piece. Woolner's black bishop at **c8** can no longer see the knight on **g4** it is defending. It is a tricky moment too for the black rook. It has to be careful where it moves for the white pawn thrusting further will leave a check on the black king from the bishop on **c4**. Did you see that?

11 .....   Qd8 – h4

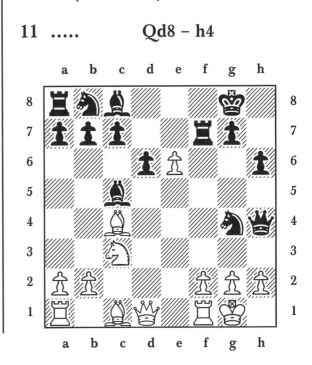

12 e6 × Rf7+

Woolner threatens mate but Charousek has regained lost material with interest. And Wollner is in check.

12 .....   Kg8 – f8

13 Bc1 – f4   mobilizing to defend mate
13 .....   Ng4 × f2
14 Qd1 – e2   threatening mate

14 .....   Nf2 – g4+ discovered check

15 Kg1 – h1   Bc8 – d7

Of course, Wollner has stopped the mate by the queen on **e8**. Charousek, however, knows the chess rule: Check out every check and capture. Look at them twice. You wouldn't have to be a potential world champion yourself to see what was coming.

16 Ra1 – e1

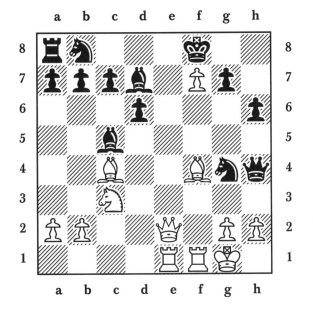

Charousek knows the rule: Bring the rooks to the center and onto open lines. He is shortly going to use them both to give mate. All great players know the rules of chess strategy.

16 ..... Nb8 – c6

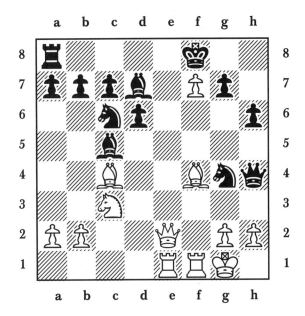

Wollner finally develops his knight and, at the same time, connects his rook to the crucial **e8** square. He "straightens his tie." Mikhail Botvinnik, a great chess world champion, always straightened his tie when he thought he was safe.

But, here, like a bolt from the blue...

Photo by Jami L. Anson, courtesy U.S. Chess Federation, New Windsor, NY 12553

17 Qe2 − e8+!!! What can you say?

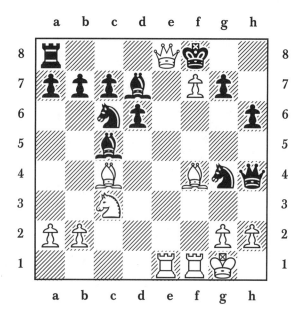

17 ..... Ra8 × e8

Wouldn't you?

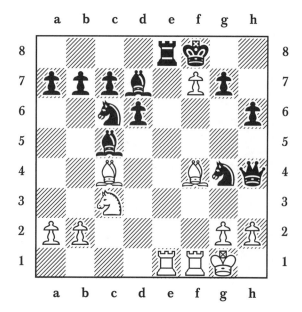

18 f7 − e8 = Q+

Puzzled? You moved your bishop to **d7** to stop this very thing! Now can you see what Charousek has had in mind for a few moves now? Double check and mate! (You saw the final position earlier in this book.)

18 .....   Bd7 × Qe8

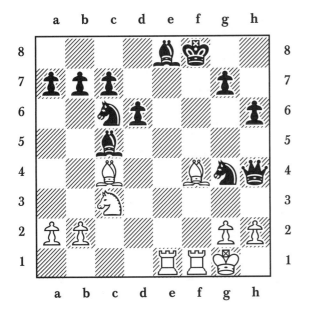

Bemused, puzzled, Wollner takes this new queen. That's why he had put the bishop in that position anyway. But now, the world class finish, or as they say in French, the "coup de grace." Can you see it? You do, I'm sure.

19   Bf4 × d6   discovered check, double check and checkmate!

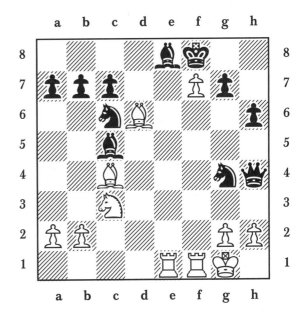

Charousek's masterful strategies have led to this final dazzling firework display of tactics.

Why not enjoy it again by setting up a board and playing through the moves below.

	WHITE	BLACK			
	Charousek	Wollner	9	Ng5 × f7	Rf8 × f7
			10	e4 – e5	Nf6 – g4
			11	e5 – e6	Qd8 – h4
1	e2 – e4	e7 – e5	12	e6 × f7+	Kg8 – f8
2	d2 – d4	e5 × d4	13	Bc1 – f4	Ng4 × f2
3	c2 – c3	d4 × c3	14	Qd1 – e2	Nf2 – g4+
4	Bf1 – c4	Ng8 – f6	15	Kg1 – h1	Bc8 – d7
5	Ng1 – f3	Bf8 – c5	16	Ra1 – e1	Nb8 – c6
6	Nb1 × c3	d7 – d6	17	Qe2 – e8+	Ra8 × e8
7	0 – 0	0 – 0	18	f7 × e8 = Q+	Bd7 × e8
8	Nf3 – g5	h7 – h6	19	Bf4 × d6++ and mate	

SOLUTIONS

TEST YOUR PROGRESS: FORK

1. **1. ..... Ne2+**, and after the king moves, **2. ..... N × Qc1**.
2. **1. ..... Bc6+, 2 Kg1 Nf3+**. And, after the king moves, **3. ..... N × Re1**, the best White can do is **3 Kf1** and take the knight, but he now has no pieces to protect his pawns.
3. **1. Qd2 × Bd5 Qd8 × Qd5 2. Nb5 – c7+** and, after the king has moved, **3. ..... Nc7 × Qd5**. No matter what he does, Black has lost a bishop!
4. **1. ..... Bc5 × f2+**. If **2. Qg3 × Bf2 Ne5 – d3+** followed by **3. ..... Nd3 × Qf2**. If **2. Ke1 × Bf2 Nf6 × e4+** followed by **3. ..... Ne4 × Qg3**. Either way Black wins the queen and at least one pawn for a bishop and knight, and leaves the white king out in the open.
5. **1. Rh4 – h8+ Kg8 × Rh8 2. Ng5 × f7+**. And after the king has moved **3. Nf7 × Qe5**.
6. **1. ..... Ka8 × Rb7 2. Nc6 – d8+** wins the queen. If Black does not take the rook or knight, then White mates him!

TEST YOUR PROGRESS: PIN

1. **1. ..... Bb4 – c5** attacks the queen. It cannot move out of the way because the king would be in check to the bishop.
2. **1. ..... Re8 × Re4+**. The pawn on **f3** cannot take the Black rook because the king will be in check to the bishop on **h5**.
3. **1. ..... Qd4 × Be4**. White loses a bishop. If **2. d3 × Qe4 Rd8 × Qd2**, White has still lost a bishop.
4. **1. Qg5 – h5+ K moves. 2. Qh5 × Qf3**.
5. **1. Rd8 – d5+**. The pawn on **c6** cannot take because the king would be in check to the queen on **e8**.
   If **1. ..... Re5× Rd5 2. Qd8 × Qd1**.
   If **1. ..... K moves, 2. Rd5 × Re5** and White wins a rook.
6. **1. ..... Qh3 × Bg3+**. The pawn on **f2** cannot take because the king would be in check to the bishop on **c5**.

TEST YOUR PROGRESS: DISCOVERED CHECK

1. **1. Ng3 – f5** or **1. Ng3 × Be4** discovered check and mate. The king is in check from the rook on **g1**. It cannot move to **h8** as it will be in check from the bishop on **a1**.
2. **1. Ne5 – c6** discovered check and then if **1. ..... Bf8 – e7** or **1. ..... Qd8 – e7 2 Nc6 × Q**.
3. **1. Rg7 – f7** discovered check and then if **1. ..... Kh8 – g8** or **1. ..... Qf8 – g7 2 Rf7 × Q**.
4. **1. ..... Qd7 – d1+**. Now if **2. Qe2 × Qd1 e3 – e2** discovered check, then if **3. Kg1 – h1 e2 × Qd1 = Q+, 4. Bc4 – f1 Qd1 × Bf1** mate.
   (If instead **3. Qd1 – d4 Bc5 × Qd4+ 4. Kg1 – h1 e2 – e1 = Q+ 5. Bc4 – f1 Qd1 × Bf1** mate.)
   If **2. Qe2 – f1 e3 – e2** discovered check **3. Kg1 – h1 Qd1 × f1** mate.
5. Five pieces at least. **1. Re7 – g7+ Kg8 – h8 2. Rg7 × Bd7** discovered check. **2. ..... Kh8 – g8 3. Rd7 – g7+ Kg8 – h8 4. Rg7 × c7** discovered check **Kh8 – g8 5. Rc7 – g7+ Kg8 – h8 6. Rg7 × b7** discovered check **Kh8 – g8 7. Rb7 – g7+ Kg8 – h8 8. Rg7 × a7** discovered check **Kh8 – g8 9 Ra7 × Ra8** and after **9. ..... Kg8 – f7** White can even take the knight for the rook and still win easily!
6. After **1. Kh1 × g2 Bg7 × Re5** discovered check, **2. K moves Be5 × Qd6**.

TEST YOUR PROGRESS: SKEWER

1. **1. ..... Ra8 – a6+ 2 Kd6 – d5** (or **c5** or **e5**) **Ra6 – a5+ 3.** K moves **Ra5 × Rh5**. Did you see that if it had been White's move, there was a mate?
2. **1. ..... Bf3 – g4+ 2.** K moves **Bg4 × Qc8**.
3. **1. ..... Rd8 – e8 2. Qe7 – a3 Re8 × Re1+**.
4. **1. ..... Qd8 – h4+ 2. Kf2 × f3 Qh4 – h5+ 3.** K moves **Qh5 × Qd1**.
5. **1. ..... Nc4 × e5+ 2. d4 × Ne5** (if **2. ..... K moves**, then **Ne5 × Qd7**). **2. ..... Qd1+ 3.** K moves **Qd1 × Qd7**.
6. **1. Ra6 – a8**. If **1. ..... Rh1 × h7 2. Ra8 – a7+** K moves. **3. Ra7 × Rh7**. The skewer threat keeps the pawn safe, and White will queen his pawn next move."

STRATEGY TIPS

Tactics are ways to make an immediate gain during play, such as forks, pins, discovered check, and the skewer. *Strategy* is the overall game plan. Chess players **must** have a plan. Plans can change, but don't make a move without first having a plan in mind!

The right game plan depends in part on the stage of the game: opening, middlegame, or endgame. After the opening, when most of the pieces move from the back squares and into the game, comes the middlegame, which lasts until either player is checkmated or most of the pieces are traded off. The endgame usually revolves around promoting a pawn to a queen.

It's often in the middlegame that a game is won or lost—and where planning is especially important! Choose a good plan and play moves that fit that plan. Use tactics to win pawns, pieces, or even to checkmate your opponent's king.

Always think about the position on the board. A plan has to fit the circumstances! Here are some planning tips.

Most important is king safety! Does your king need more protection? Is your opponent's king safe? Can they be attacked successfully? The object of chess is to checkmate the opponent's king; keep yours safe! Castle into safety behind a wall of pawns, and keep your pawns in front of your king unmoved if possible —they're strongest that way.

If your opponent's king is not safely protected, your plan could be to attack it! A good attack plan calls for gathering a strong force—a number of chess pieces—to assault the other king. One or two pieces aren't normally enough.

Control the center or attack your opponent's grip on it. Remember "King of the Mountain," where each player tries to occupy and keep control of the top of a hill? The center is the "high ground" of the chess board! To travel around the board, pieces must pass through the center. The player who has control of it has a tremendous advantage! Occupy the center if you can. If your opponent has control, try to undermine it!

Make sure your pieces guard or defend one another, even if they are not immediately attacked. Try to guard your pieces with chessmen of equal or less value.

If possible, trade a piece for a more valuable one. Soon your army will be more powerful than your opponent's. Be careful what you trade for.

What is my opponent threatening? Ask yourself this each time your opponent moves. Credit your opponent for having a game plan of his or her own! If you see threats coming, you can usually avoid them.

Position your men for maximum control of the board. By moving pawns, will I make one of my bishop's "bad"? Your bishops should be very powerful, board-sweeping pieces. Avoid the common mistake of "locking up" a bishop behind a wedge of pawns on the same color squares as the bishop. This locks a so-called "bad" bishop out of the game!

Here, the short-range but jumping knight is much more powerful than the opposing bishop because it can get around the board; the "locked" bishop can't!

Try to keep your pawns "healthy." Pawns are the only chessmen that cannot move backwards, so they are vulnerable. They should be in a position to defend each other whenever possible.

Keep pawns connected; without "holes" between them. Isolated pawns are weak because they cannot protect each other. Black easily wins the end game at right.

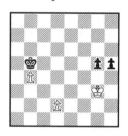

Also, avoid "doubling" pawns—placing them on the same file. If one pawn is blocking another, behind it, they are both weaker than "healthy" pawns, those that are able to protect one another. White easily wins the end game above.

A pawn that is behind its neighboring pawns, is called "backward." It is weak because its neighbors cannot defend it!

In the middlegame, pawns should capture towards the center. Count your change! Consider center pawns (in front of kings or queens as the game starts) as worth a dollar, pawns in front of bishops (bishop pawns) 90 cents, pawns in front of knights 80 cents, and those in front of rooks only 70 cents. So the general rule is to try to capture towards the center (here **h2 × g3**).

Note: These pawn values hold only for the middlegame! In the endgame, a pawn far from the kings *can* be the most valuable chesspiece on the board—marching forward to become a queen!

Put your rooks and queens—your most powerful pieces—on open or "semi-open" files. Files are "open" when there are no pawns on them. Files are "semi-open" when only one side has a pawn on it. Rooks, and often queens, need to be on such files to exert the most influence.

If you and your opponent have castled on opposite sides, think "pawn storm." When your opponent is castled on the other side of the board from your own king, you might want to move your pawns towards his king. Even if some are captured, open files will be created in front of his king and you'll be able to put your rooks on these files to help your attack.

Always review your possible moves before making a decision. Figure out what two or three moves seem best in the position. Make a mental list of these moves, then consider each of them one at a time. Finally, decide on one.

CERTIFICATE OF ACHIEVEMENT

This is to certify that _____

having read the book *Winning Chess Tactics and Strategies*,

and completed and passed its tests and challenges, including:

The King and Two

Bishops Vs. King

Mating Race

and the

Test Your Progress Quizzes

has earned this honorable

Certificate of Achievement, signed and hereby

presented by the authors:

Ted Nottingham,
Bob Wade
and Al Lawrence

Ted Nottingham
Bob Wade
Al Lawrence

Attested to and signed by:

_____   _____

Name   Date

INDEX

Age, starting, of masters, 92
Adli, al-, 5
Alekhine, Alexander, 93, 108
Algebraic notation, short, 57
Anand, Viswanath, 48, 53

Bacrot, Etienne, 64
"Bad bishop," 124
Bishops, opposite-color, 85
Bogolyubov, Ewfim, 29
Botvinnik, Mikhail, 59, 93
Byrne, Donald, 49

Capablanca, José Raúl, 28,
    29–31, 32–34, 89–92, 93
Castle, 5, 12, 82
Center control, 124
Certificate form, 125
Charousek, Rudolf, 47, 58,
    114–115, 116–121
Chess board, folding, 12
Chigorin, Mikhail, 115
Churchill, Winston, 93

Dark bishop, 80
"Deep Blue," 48
Did You Know?, 5, 12, 13,
    28, 29, 64, 107
Draw, 78, 85
Double check, 58
Dream start, 12–13
Duel for queen game, 7–11

Endgame trick, 106
Euwe, Max, 93
Family fork, royal, 31

FIDE (Fédération Internatio-
    nale des Echecs) , 34, 35
Fischer, Robert G. (Bobby),
    48, 49, 93
Fork, knight, 26–27
Forks, 26–37
Fuller, Max, 53–57

Gambit, 116
Game plan, 83
Gibaud, Amédée, 17
Gibaud vs. Lazard, 16, 17,
    17–20
Göttingen manuscript, 13
Gunsberg, Isidor, 94–107

Handbook of Chess Openings,
    The, 115
Havasi, Kornel, 29

"In-between" move, 88

Jorgensen, Walter, 5

Karpov, Anatoly, 34, 48
Kasparov, Garry, 48–49, 53,
    65–68
Keats, John, 94, 115
King, 62–72
Knight
    checkmate, 32–34
    fork, 26–27
    improving play, 89–91
Korchnoi, Victor, 64
Kostich, Boris, 92
Lasker, Emanuel, 93, 94,

    114–115
Law, Bonar, 28
Lays of Ancient Rome, 93
Lazard, Fred, 17
Legal, Sire de, 14–16
Legal's Mate, 14
Leko, Peter, 64
Lessing–Rosenwald tourna-
    ment, 49
Lucena manuscript, 5, 13

Mating race, 71–80, 80
"Meister," 29
Memory test, 93
Mephisto, 94–95
Middlegame, 122
Mieses, Jacques, 29
Morphy, Paul, 93, 94, 116
Murray, Harold James
    Ruthven, 64

Notation, 57, 78
Nunn, John, 48, 59

Oxford History of Chess, 64

Pachman, Ludek, 116
"Passed" pawn, 94
"Pawn storm," 124
Pawns, "healthy," 124
Penrose, Jonathan, 53, 57
Petrosian, Tigran, 93
Philidor, André, 107
Piece strategies,
    bishop, 82–84
    king, 92

knight, 89–91
queen, 87–88
rook, 85–86
Pillsbury, Harry Nelson,
    93–94, 94–107
Pin, 38–41, 42–44, 45–46
Polgar, Judith, 34–35, 64

Queen, later entrance, 21
Queen's Pawn Opening, 81

Rashid, Harun al-, 64
Reti, Richard, 28
Robot, chess-playing, *See*
    Mephisto *and* Gunsberg,
    Isidor
Royal family fork, 31
Ruy López opening, 13

Saavedra, Pedro, 28
Saint Brie, 14–16

Shirov, Alexey, 34–35
Short, Nigel, 48, 53–57
Sire de Legal vs. Saint Brie,
    14–16
Skewer, 64–66, 68, 69–70
Smothered mate, 34
Smyslov, Vassily, 93
Sorensen, 5
Spassky, Boris, 64, 90, 93
Stages of game, 123
Stalemate, *See* Draw
Staunton, Howard, 53
Steinitz, Wilhelm, 93
Strategy tips, 123–124
Suli, al-, 64

Tactics vs. strategy, 123
Tal, Mikhail, 93
Tatai, Stefano, 65–67
Test Your Progress quizzes
    discovered check, 60–61

fork, 36–37
pin, 45–46
skewer, 69–70
(solutions: 122)

United States Chess Federa-
    tion, 7

Value of pawns, 124

West, Guy, 49–52
Wollner, J., 58, 116–121
World Chess Council (WCC),
    47
World Chess Federation, *See*
    FIDE

Yanofsky, Abe, 108–113

Zapata, Alonso, 59
Zwischenzug, 88

About the Authors

British school teacher **Ted Nottingham** captured the imagination of the public and the attention of the media when he coached his small village school to the British National Championships. He is the architect of the "Lincolnshire" method, which uses small, logical steps and reinforcing exercises that are both effective and fun, while integrating chess and its famous personalities into a wider context of history and world events. As a child, Nottingham had a special interest in picking horses to win the Derby (see page 114). Twice county chess champion of Lincolnshire and South Humberside, Ted Nottingham lives in Spalding, England.

Al Lawrence, now president of the OutExcel! Corporation, was Executive Director of the United States Chess Federation during a decade of record-breaking growth. An expert chess player and a former public school and college teacher with advanced degrees in instructional techniques, he writes widely on chess and other topics. He makes his home in Wallkill, New York.

Bob Wade, Officer of the Order British Empire, is three-time champion of New Zealand and two-time champion of Great Britain. In 1950 he was awarded the title International Master by the World Chess Federation (FIDE). He is widely considered one of the most eminent scholars in the field of chess. He lives in London, surrounded by piles of chess books and manuscripts.